Doorways to the Sacred

ANCIENT FAITH, FUTURE MISSION

Doorways to the Sacred

Developing Sacramentality in Fresh Expressions of Church

Edited by
Phil Potter
and
Ian Mobsby

CANTERBURY PRESS
Norwich

Published in 2017 by Canterbury Press
Editorial office
3rd Floor, Invicta House,
108–114 Golden Lane,
London EC1Y 0TG, UK

Canterbury Press is an imprint of Hymns Ancient & Modern Ltd
(a registered charity)

Hymns Ancient & Modern® is a registered trademark of
Hymns Ancient & Modern Ltd
13A Hellesdon Park Road, Norwich,
Norfolk NR6 5DR, UK

British Library Cataloguing in Publication data

A catalogue record for this book is available
from the British Library

978 1 84825 951 5

Typeset by Manila Typesetting
Printed and bound by
CPI Group (UK) Ltd, Croydon

Contents

The Contributors

Susan Blagden is Diocesan Training Officer for St Padarn's Institute in the Church in Wales, and is involved in training and formation of all those seeking licensed ministry within the Church. She is also an Oblate of St Mary the Virgin, Wantage, and a Companion with Contemplative Fire. She is a photographer and founder of www.contemplativecamera.org. She leads retreats and quiet days exploring the twin themes of contemplative prayer and photography.

Adrian Chatfield is an Anglican priest and theological educator whose ministry has taken him to five provinces in four continents. He has been engaged in new and experimental ways of being and doing church for 48 years and, until 2014, was a member of the national Fresh Expressions core team. As a tutor at Ridley Hall, he helped set up the Contextual Training Pathway, shared in pioneer training and mentoring, and remains part of the Centre for Pioneer Learning. Now living in Ilkeston, Derbyshire, he continues to offer spiritual direction and mentoring to pioneers, is involved with pioneer training in the Diocese of Derby, and is looking forward to helping colleagues and friends explore a more sacramental understanding of the Christian faith in new contexts.

Jonathan Clark is the Bishop of Croydon in the Diocese of Southwark. His involvement with experimental forms of church began with his membership of the Holy Joes community. Later, as Rector of Stoke Newington, he was the mission accompanier to the Moot Community, a sacramental and contemplative missional community in the City of London. He is a former Rector General of the Society of Catholic Priests, Chair of Affirming Catholicism and Chair of the Fresh Expressions Roundtable for the development of sacramental and contemplative fresh expressions of church. He continues to play an active part in leading the development of fresh expressions of church in the Diocese of Southwark and beyond.

Graham Cray is an Honorary Assistant Bishop in the Diocese of York, the Diocesan Advocate for Pioneer Ministry and Fresh Expressions of Church and Chair of the Oversight Group of Wydale Hall, the diocesan conference and retreat centre. He is the Chair of Trustees for Soul Survivor, and patron of SOMA UK. Graham was previously the Archbishops' Missioner and Leader of the Fresh Expressions team, Bishop of Maidstone, Principal of Ridley Hall and Vicar of St Michael le Belfrey in York. For four years he was chairman of the Greenbelt Festival. Graham chaired the working party that wrote the *Mission-shaped Church* (Church House Publishing, 2004) report and was a contributing author and editor of two volumes in the Ancient Faith Future Mission book series. Other publications include *Youth Congregations and the Emerging Church* (Grove Evangelism Series, 2002), *Making Sense of Generation Y: The World View of 15- to 25-year-olds* (with Bob Mayo, Sylvie Collins and Sara Savage, Church House Publishing, 2006), *Disciples and Citizens: A Vision for Distinctive Living* (Inter-Varsity Press, 2007). Graham continues in teaching, speaking and writing, retaining close links to South Africa and the USA. The core of Graham's interest lies in the renewal of the Church for mission and the encounter between gospel and culture.

Bryony Davis is an Anglican priest and until recently was chaplain at HMP/YOI Bronzefield. She was ordained in 2002 following a career as an occupational therapist, and worked as a priest in the dioceses of St Edmundsbury and Ipswich and Guildford. She currently shares in the leadership of holy::ground, Woking, a small missional community which values creativity, contemplation, community and working for justice and peace. holy::ground's installations have regularly featured at the Greenbelt Festival, where Bryony has also been a speaker. Working to improve support for women leaving prison is an important part of her life, and she has recently trained as a Restorative Justice Facilitator.

John Drane is a Trustee and member of the ecumenical board overseeing fresh expressions in the UK, and Chair of its *Mission-shaped Ministry* board. He has been on the staff of the universities of Stirling and Aberdeen, and is currently an Affiliate Professor of Practical Theology at Fuller Seminary and Fellow of St John's College Durham. He is Co-Chair (with the Bishop of Lichfield) of the Church of England's Mission Theology Advisory Group and regularly acts as a consultant with churches of different denominations on matters relating to culture, mission and theological education. His many books include the best-selling *Introducing the New Testament* (Lion Hudson, 2010), now in its third edition, and *The McDonaldization of the Church: Spirituality, Creativity and the Future of The Church* (Darton, Longman & Todd, 2000).

Olive Fleming Drane studied at the Graduate Theological Union in San Francisco and the University of Aberdeen, and is currently an Affiliate Professor of Mission and Evangelism at Fuller Theological Seminary, California, and a Fellow of St John's College Durham. She is a member of the ecumenical group encouraging the development of fresh expressions in the Scottish churches, and has also worked with theological colleges and churches of various traditions in Australia as they explore their missional vision. Her previous research into the spiritual practices of ordinary people in Europe and the USA inspired the publication of *Spirituality to Go: Rituals and Reflections for Everyday Living* (Darton, Longman & Todd, 2006). She is also the author of *Clowns, Storytellers, Disciples: Spirituality and Creativity for Today's Church* (Bible Reading Fellowship and Augsburg Fortress Publishing, 2004), and created the worship resources for the *Mission-shaped Ministry* course.

Julie Leger Dunstan is Director for Formation and Professional Development at the London Centre for Spiritual Direction, which includes oversight of Encounter, the London Course in Spiritual Direction. She is a licensed lay-minister at All Saints, West Dulwich where she relishes her role as Deacon and preacher. She has a particular interest in bridging spiritual direction and the Church, promoting the conversation between the interior life and the gospels, and is passionate about the resources of liturgy and sacrament for the spiritual life and faith. She is an Oblate at St Mary's Abbey in West Malling.

Stephen Hance is Canon Missioner at Southwark Cathedral and Director of Mission and Evangelism for the Diocese of Southwark. Prior to this he served in churches in Balham, Islington and Portsmouth. He trained for the ordained ministry at St John's Nottingham, and has degrees in theology, leadership and sociology. He is the founder of the Cathedrals and Growth Network, and is a member of the General Synod of the Church of England. He is a contributor to *How to Do Mission Action Planning: Prayer, Process and Practice* (Mike Chew and Mark Ireland, SPCK, 2016) and has written on confirmation and parenting (Bible Reading Fellowship).

Kim Hartshorne is a former engineer and charity worker who, with a small group of housewives, started the Upper Room in 2008, a drop-in centre and experimental space to meet and pray with people who were far off from Church. Influenced by the 24/7 prayer movement, the Upper Room became the first 'Bishop's Mission Order' (allowing partnership between parishes) of the Diocese of Gloucester. Kim is now an ordained Pioneer Minister who leads this fresh expression of church, which continues to explore how liturgy can be helpful and appropriate in the faith journeys of people who may be homeless, struggle with mental illness or learning disability or be unable to read confidently.

Reagan Humber is an ordained Episcopal priest and pastor at House for All Sinners and Saints, a missional congregation in Denver, Colorado, of the Evangelical Lutheran Church in America. Reagan has worked closely with Nadia Bolz-Weber as the founder and Theologian. Together Reagan and Nadia have led what started as a mission project into a full expression of church.

Ian Mobsby is the Mission Enabler to the Woolwich Episcopal Area of the Diocese of Southwark and part-time Priest in Charge of the Parish of St Luke's Camberwell in Peckham, South London. He has a background of involvement in four different missional communities including the Moot Community in the City of London and is currently the Prior to the Wellspring New Monastic Missional Community in Peckham. He is an international writer and speaker with a number of books including work on New Monasticism and the Holy Trinity in mission and contemporary spirituality. Ian is an Associate Missioner of the Fresh Expressions Movement in the UK and a national selector for pioneer ministry in the Church of England. He has a background in speaking and writing in the area of mission, evangelism and contemporary culture in Australia, New Zealand, Canada, the USA, Europe and the UK, and is an associate lecturer in a number of theological institutes including St Augustine's College in England. For more information on Ian, see www.stlukespeckham.co.uk or www.ianmobsby.net. Ian is currently doing a PhD exploring how the Church can respond to those who are unchurched and 'spiritual not religious'.

Mike Moynagh is based at Wycliffe Hall, Oxford, and is Consultant on Theology and Practice to the Fresh Expressions in the UK team. He has written extensively about new and emerging forms of church, including *Church for Every Context* (SCM Press, 2012), which has become a leading academic textbook, and *Being Church, Doing Life* (Monarch, 2014). He is currently writing *Church in Life* (forthcoming, SCM Press, 2017), a follow-up to his 2012 book. He lectures and teaches widely on the subject in the UK and overseas.

Lucy Moore is leader of the Messy Church team at The Bible Reading Fellowship, and is involved in the leadership of a Messy Church. Lucy speaks at local and national events, and is a passionate promoter of lay vocations in the Church, and currently a member of the Church of England Liturgical Commission to help the Church of England adapt to enabling forms of worship that are sympathetic to missional communities.

Phil Potter is the Archbishops' Missioner and UK national Team Leader of fresh expressions of church. Before this, he was Director of Pioneer Ministry in the Diocese of Liverpool, where one in three parishes has now planted at least one fresh expression of church. He has also been involved for the past few years in national and international strategies for promoting new ways of doing church, and in the recent past has worked as a consultant and speaker in Australasia, North America, Finland, Denmark, Norway and Germany. For 20 years, he led his local church through many transitions, from being a traditional urban congregation to a large and vibrant mixed economy Cell Church, able to resource and encourage others with its story of renewal, reordering, restructuring and reinventing. He has written two books: *Pioneering a New Future*, formerly published as *The Challenge of Change* (Bible Reading Fellowship, 2009/15), and *The Challenge of Cell Church* (Bible Reading Fellowship, 2001).

Philip Roderick delights in the natural world, human creativity and lifelong learning. On a quest for God in the early 1970s, Philip explored different faith paths. While at a Sufi community in Gloucestershire, he experienced a conversion to Christ. A stay in an experimental Christian community run by Fr Slade of the Cowley Fathers opened his eyes to different ways of praying – with the body, with symbol, poetry, stillness and biblical chant. Philip then spent a year in a Russian Orthodox hermitage in the UK. His time as University Chaplain and lecturer in Theology at Bangor University, as Principal of a lay training scheme in the Diocese of Oxford, together with his subsequent work as a parish priest in Amersham and Spirituality Adviser in Sheffield, created fertile ground for the three ministries Philip has initiated: The Quiet Garden Movement, www.quietgarden.org, Contemplative Fire, www.contemplativefire.org, and Hidden Houses of Prayer.

Simon Sutcliffe is an activist, ordained Methodist Minister and reflective missional practitioner who is involved in leading a fresh expression of church as part of the Methodist Venture FX Scheme. He also helps lead the Methodist Pioneering Pathways for Methodist Pioneers and is tutor in Evangelism and Pioneering Ministries at the Queen's Theological Foundation in Birmingham. Simon has also begun researching a theology of *guesthood* as a resource for mission.

Sue Wallace is the Canon Precentor and Sacrist at Winchester Cathedral, with experience of involvement in Alternative Worship and Fresh Expressions of Church. She has a background in music technology and video art and as an ordained priest has served in York and Leeds. For 15 years Sue led the Visions Community in York and ran the Transcendence Ancient-Future mass in York Minster.

Karen Ward is an Episcopal priest and self-described 'domestic missionary' in the USA, now serving in the Episcopal Diocese of Oregon, as vicar/redeveloper of St Andrew and All Souls Episcopal Church and Founder and Director of Portland Abbey Arts in Portland, Oregon. Karen is widely known as a leader in the Emerging Church Movement in the USA, and was the Founding Pastor and Developer of Church of the Apostles, Seattle, and the Co-Founder of the Fremont Abbey Arts Center, Seattle. Karen has contributed a number of chapters in this Ancient Faith Future Mission book series.

Introduction

PHIL POTTER AND IAN MOBSBY

Fresh expressions of church are now key to the mission strategies of most of the historic denominations in the UK and beyond. Some of the great challenges and questions concern how fresh expressions evolve from being a form of mission project through to becoming mature expressions of the Church. Developing a sacramental life in each fresh expression is very important if mission initiatives are going to grow into healthy ecclesial communities. Further, a number of sacraments are missional in and of themselves. This book therefore seeks to engage with the question 'What would the rhythm of a sacramental life look like in a healthy, maturing fresh expression of church given its context?' This will seek to resource pioneers, missioners and evangelists who are heading up a fresh expression of church. Further we also seek to support 'overseers' of local fresh expressions, including parish, deanery, circuit or congregational clergy or pastors who are seeking wisdom in how to do this well.

With this in mind, this book seeks to provide stories and theological reflection about how this can be approached and facilitated in practice. This addresses a broad understanding of the sacraments of the Church, which in reality vary between the different denominations. St Augustine, in the fifth century, defined a sacrament or, in his words a *mysterion*, as 'a visible sign of an invisible reality'.[1] As such, sacraments are seen as the work of God the Holy Spirit working through the churches as ordained by Christ. In the Anglican Book of Common Prayer a sacrament is defined as:

> an outward and visible sign of an inward and spiritual grace given unto us, ordained by Christ himself, as a means whereby we receive the same, and a pledge to assure us thereof.[2]

Depending on your denomination and church tradition, what is officially a sacrament varies in number between none, two and seven. Some see the official sacraments as baptism and Holy Communion, believing the other five are more 'sacramentals' and by implication less important, or not sacraments. Those of a more catholic or sacramental tradition will acknowledge seven as official sacraments and no 'sacramentals'. For the purposes of this book, a broad understanding of seven sacraments is assumed (where five may be 'sacramentals' depending on your tradition), which are important to express in a fresh expression of church. These seven are baptism, confirmation, Eucharist or Holy Communion, confession or reconciliation, anointing the sick for healing, ordination and marriage. This book explores the importance of the first five of these sacraments as particular challenges for missional communities coming from different ecumenical perspectives. This is not to in any way undermine the sacraments of ordination and marriage. It is the editors' view that these are already covered by a substantial number of publications. So chapters in this book explore the place of sacraments in missional forms of the Church and also increasingly their place in the world. We listen to the wisdom of a mix of theologians and reflective pioneer practitioners drawing on the stories of various fresh expressions in the UK and USA, and how they have approached the issue of building sacramentalism into their pattern of worship, mission and community. Further we hear how sacraments by themselves can be used missionally, often by implication rediscovering their place in the complexity of the modern world.

The process then of building sacraments into the life of something that begins as a project and grows into a form of church is less than straightforward. Steven Croft helpfully calls this 'building an ecclesial community out of contextual mission'.[3]

So in this evolutionary process, it is critical that the leader of a particular fresh expression knows when a form of sacramentality becomes important, and is fully involved in prayer and discernment to begin to explore how this can be contextualized. Helpfully this evolutionary process is named in the definition of a fresh expression, and as expressed in Figure 1:

> A fresh expression of church is a form of church for our changing culture established primarily for the benefit of people who are not yet members of any church. It will come into being through principles of listening, service, incarnational mission and making disciples. It will have the potential to become a mature expression of church shaped by the gospel and the enduring marks of the church and for its cultural context.[4]

Drawing on this definition and illustration it is clear to see that consideration of developing a sacramentality emerges as an issue between the third and sixth circles (building community and church taking shape). If working with 'de-and-unchurched' people this will clearly begin with the two sacraments of initiation (baptism and confirmation) as 'becoming Christian' and then Holy Communion or Eucharist as a definitive sign of 'becoming Church'. The skill and art of leading a fresh expression is to hold onto a form of triple listening – to God in prayer, to the specific context and ecclesial community, and to the Bible and Church tradition. It is crucial that the process of contextualization does not just impose a sacramental form

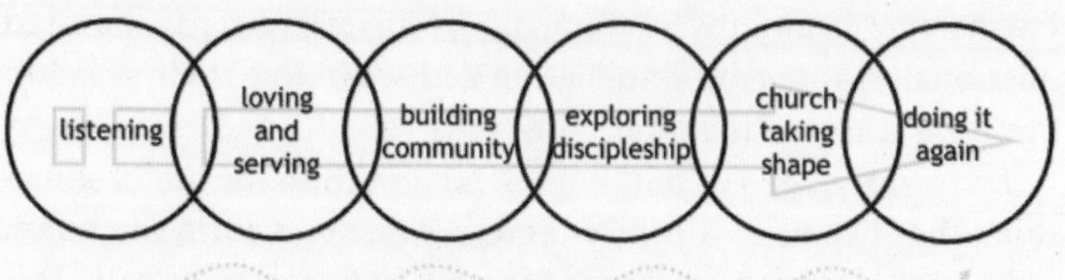

Figure 1: Fresh expressions developmental process.[5]

without this contextual listening. It should be expected that the Holy Spirit will unsettle a community, or cause the need for sacramentalism to emerge in the life of the fresh expression of church. Further, it is important that the leader of the fresh expression works accountably to and with overseers and participants. For example, in the Church of England there is permission to explore the contextualization of different forms of liturgy where there is a proven pastoral need so to do, and the leader of the fresh expression rightly should seek permission of the bishop or archdeacon not only for accountability purposes, but also to allow the Church to learn from such developmental work.

Given the complexity of being a fresh expression of church, it is the editors' view that this sacramental need will not end with the establishment of baptism, confirmation and Holy Communion. In addition all the other sacraments and sacramentals need consideration in response to ill-health, relational and community conflict, vocational development, marriage, death and dying. Again these need to be considered contextually and also in how they relate to the particular church tradition.

In response to these needs, this book is divided into five parts, each relating to differing aspects of sacramentalism. Each part is introduced by the editors to help the reader to make connections with potential points of learning.

Part 1, 'Sacraments in Context and Culture', includes chapters from Graham Cray, Olive Drane and John Drane. Graham addresses theological concerns raised by some in response to the development of fresh expressions sacramentality while Olive and John explore how sacramentalism can grow out of creativity and contemporary culture.

In Part 2, 'Sacraments in Formation and Worship', Stephen Hance explores the connection between creative liturgy and sacrament, while Reagan Humber explores how a particular fresh expression in Denver Colorado grew a sacramentalism by creative engagement with the sacraments and contemporary culture. Reagan's chapter also touches on considerations for those who have had bad experiences of church, commonly called the 'de-churched'.

Part 3, 'Sacraments in Initiation', includes chapters from Jonathan Clark, Susan Blagden and Philip Roderick on baptism and Ian Mobsby on confirmation.

Part 4, 'Sacraments in Eucharist and Holy Communion', includes chapters exploring the stories of a number of different fresh expressions by Lucy Moore, Sue Wallace, Karen Ward, and Kim Hartshorne.

Part 5, 'Sacraments in Healing, Confession and Reconciliation', includes chapters from Adrian Chatfield, Bryony Davis, Julie Leger Dunstan and Simon Sutcliffe. Adrian's chapter opens up the whole issue of considering a sacrament of healing in a highly technological culture of 'cures'. Bryony's chapter reminds us of the great need for sensitivity with those whose lives are full of shame and broken dreams, while Julie's chapter builds on the theme of confession, drawing on the insights of spiritual direction, before Simon's chapter reflects on the importance of reconciliation, crucial for when missional communities face serious conflict or 'go wrong'.

Finally, we asked Michael Moynagh to write an Afterword drawing on his reflections on all the preceding chapters.

The editors wish to express their gratitude to Canterbury Press and in particular to Christine Smith for her ongoing support for this book in the continuing Ancient Faith Future Mission series, and to all the willing authors who have given up substantial amounts of their time to make this happen. We hope you the reader will be inspired, challenged and encouraged by the wisdom and insights of this book, to help develop mature fresh expressions of church which draw on a deep sacramentalism that in turn increases the effective mission and renewal of the Church in the UK, USA and beyond.

Notes

1 Guilherme Oliveira, *Saint Augustine and Sacramental Theology*, Academia.edu, USA, as downloaded in 2016 from www.academia.edu/3663552/Saint_Augustine_and_Sacramental_Theology.

2 From the Catechism from the Book of Common Prayer from www.churchofengland.org/prayer-worship/worship/book-of-common-prayer/a-catechism.aspx.

3 Steven Croft and Ian Mobsby (eds), *Ancient Faith Future Mission: Fresh Expressions in the Sacramental Tradition*, Canterbury Press, Norwich, 2012.

4 Steven Croft, *Mission-shaped Questions: Defining Issues for Today's Church*, Church House Publishing, London, 2008, p. 9.

5 Michael Moynagh, *A Fresh Expressions Journey – A Rationale*, as downloaded in 2016 from www.freshexpressions.org.uk/guide/develop/rationale.

PART I

Sacraments in Context and Culture

God has made known to us the mystery of God's will, according to God's good pleasure that God set forth in Christ, and how the mystery was made known to me by revelation, as I wrote above in a few words, and to make everyone see what is the plan of the mystery hidden for ages in God who created all things. (Ephesians 1.9, 3.3, 3.9)

Introduction

Olive Drane's Chapter 3 sets the scene that sacramentality begins with creativity as the outworking of the Holy Spirit, and that this sacramentality begins in the world. The reader should note that the sacraments don't start in church, but begin with the presence of God the Holy Spirit in contemporary culture. John Drane's Chapter 2 reminds us again that even in a post-religious culture, many are still deeply searching for spirituality and significance, and that the sacraments have a lot to do with spiritual and transformational experience. Lots of great wisdom here from Olive and John.

Graham Cray's Chapter 1 not only stresses how important the development of a sacramentality is for fresh expressions of church, but he goes further to share some wisdom. Rightly he recognizes the categories of pilgrims, seekers and suppressors, and how fresh expressions are often focused on these last two groupings, along with the challenge of holding the tension of being an ecclesial community with the need to let 'de-and-unchurched' people 'belong before they believe'. Graham engages with the need to consider a sacramental development, of making new paths to take unchurched people forward through a process that recognizes the different stages of being an enquirer, initiate through to being a disciple. This requires prayerful discernment, and great skill to map out this development, particularly in terms of an emerging sacramentality as the fresh expression shifts from being a mission project to missional church.

I

Doors to the Sacred through Fresh Expressions of Church

GRAHAM CRAY

A question has been raised about the validity of 'fresh expressions of church'. How can they be authentic expressions of the Church if they do not minister the dominical sacraments? The challenge is fair but shows little understanding of the missionary context in which fresh expressions are established, nor the process of planting them, including the establishing of sacramental life. Forty per cent of those attending fresh expressions of church in the Church of England have no previous history with any church. The establishment of church life for them, including sacramental life, involves both a culture of 'belonging before believing' and a form of catechumenate. This chapter will demonstrate how fresh expressions open doors to the sacred for those who have never previously engaged with them.

The primary purpose of fresh expressions of church is to gain, as Christian disciples, those who have no connection to the Church, and who are unlikely to be drawn into more traditional congregations. The good news from the research carried out across ten dioceses is that, from the leaders' perspective, 40% of those attending had never had any significant church experience, and a further 35% had once been involved in a church, some just as children, some as adults, but were no longer attending.[1] The fresh expressions movement appears to be succeeding in its primary aim. But the aim is more than attendance. It is committed discipleship in Christ's church. To make disciples, and to be authentic expressions of the Christian

Church, fresh expressions of church must develop an appropriate practice of sacramental life. But the critics who make this point often fail to understand either the process required, or the issues involved in that development.

The sacraments of the Christian Church were famously described by the Roman Catholic theologian Joseph Martos as 'Doors to the Sacred'.[2] This chapter will largely limit itself to the dominical sacraments of baptism and Holy Communion, but Martos is right, the sacraments are doors to the sacred, to the reality of the gospel of Jesus Christ in his church. Sadly, for much of the population of the UK, these are overgrown doors, concealed at the end of long disused footpaths. To pilot men, women and children, with no prior experience of church, along these footpaths and through those doors requires patience, faith and openness to change. For this reason fresh expressions do not normally start with a public worship service, but with engagement with a community rooted in prayerful listening.

Overgrown doors

Part of the responsibility for the cultural and spiritual gap between the Church, and those who have no connection with it, lies with the local church.

It might simply be an issue of hospitality and welcome. It is easy to confuse the ease we have with those with whom we have worshipped regularly, with hospitality to newcomers. The one is no guarantee of the other. This is a key missional issue, as hospitality lies at the heart of the gospel.[3] We are recipients and beneficiaries of God's costly hospitality, through his Son. However, lack of hospitality can be addressed easily if there is the will to do so.[4] The answer is not necessarily to plant a fresh expression of church. Most churches could expand the range of people they reach by better attention to invitation, welcome and hospitality.

But the problem can be more serious. The church is an incarnational community. It is called to embody Christ, to be the body of Christ, in a particular locality.[5] As it embodies Christ in that place, it is sign, instrument and foretaste of God's purposes for that place.[6] So when a congregation loses touch with its community, or parts of its community, it has departed from its vocation, by failing to be incarnational. This is often because the locality has changed, but the congregation has not. Such change is gradual. It is only noticeable over time. But the consequence can be a church culture alien to the current community (for all the wrong reasons), or a museum piece, simply preserving the way things used to be. Loyal, but more mission minded, members of the congregation acknowledge that they are attending services to which they could never bring a friend. Worship and everyday life become divorced. If the situation is long term it can have serious consequences. 'Our lack of inculturation (embodying Christ in culture) has fostered both the cultural alienation of some Christians, and an over-ready willingness of others to live in two cultures, one of their religion and the other of their everyday life.'[7]

Such congregations may still serve those who do attend very well. Lack of inculturation is not the same as lack of spiritual vitality. They will often be capable of adding new members from their own generation, or cultural group. But mission to the locality may require a mixed economy approach, by complementing the existing congregation with a fresh expression.

Not all church doors are overgrown. Sadly the exit doors are well used, as considerable numbers of people have left their churches over recent decades.[8] But there is hope: 35% of the attendance of fresh expressions of church in ten Church of England dioceses are 'de-churched', people returning, in addition to the 40% who were never part of a church. Some new doors are being opened.

Disused footpaths

Some half of the population of England has had little regular contact with any church, even as children.[9] Footpaths to Christian faith and Christian worship, well known to previous generations, are unknown to them. Nor is it simply a matter of erecting some new signposts. Important though it is that we be an inviting church,[10] many people outside the Church have little that would motivate them to accept, were they to be invited.

These unchurched people have been identified as three groups within the British public. First, there are a few 'pilgrims', eclectic seekers in search of a spirituality. There is no real difficulty in engaging these extensively about spirituality. But the problem is that they are often allergic to any exclusive commitment to one particular pathway, be it the Christian faith or any other. Some seem to prefer the journey to the destination. Second, there are a larger number of 'seekers', on a therapeutic quest, looking for healing more than spirituality. 'The contemporary climate is therapeutic not religious. People hunger not for personal salvation . . . but for the feeling, the momentary illusion, of personal well-being, health and psychic security.'[11] The 'seekers' may well be engaged by the gospel through sacramental ministry – the Church's ministry of healing – whether in a charismatic or more catholic form. 'Healing On the Streets', Christian engagement in Mind, Body and Spirit fairs, and the growing interest in retreats all provide appropriate points of contact. But third, the majority he describes as 'suppressors', those who have a God-given capacity to engage with the spiritual and the transcendent, but have no knowledge of how to use it, and therefore ignore it.[12] The primary missional challenge is how to engage with this majority group. Humans made in the image of God have an innate ability to engage with God, and a potential desire for transcendence, but whether that has been suppressed or diverted by sin, or simply never activated, the question is how to engage it.

St Paul wrote that 'the god of this world has blinded the minds of the unbelievers, to keep them from seeing the light of the gospel of the glory of Christ, who is the image of God' (2 Corinthians 4.4). The 'world' here represents the way a culture works to provide a plausible world view and way of life, which makes the Christian faith seem implausible or irrelevant. Cultures are habit-forming, disciple-making entities. Our Western consumer culture provides a counterfeit transcendence that inoculates many people against the real thing.[13]

Both modernity and postmodernity are reductionist. Modernity reduced questions of purpose to questions of cause and effect. Postmodernity's individualism and relativism reduces them to pragmatism: what works for me. Neither has room for a grand narrative about God's purposes for the whole human race.

Research into 'Generation Y'[14] revealed contentment with a 'happy midi-narrative' in which, 'This world and all life in it, is meaningful as it is; there is no need to think of significance as being somewhere else.'[15] Each individual's family and friends were seen to be the only necessary resource. There was no awareness of a 'God-shaped gap' longing to be filled. 'These results do not lead us to think many young people are involved in a great deal of spiritual searching.'[16] From a Christian perspective the 'happy midi-narrative' is a (largely) contented two-dimensional life, which is unaware of the possibilities of three-dimensional life in Christ. The Eucharist is the core Christian celebration of life in God in three dimensions. Linking our lives to Christ's' past, present and future. 'Christ has died. Christ is risen. Christ will come again.'[17] Generation Y needs Christ and his community's meal. The question is how to introduce them to it.

The Generation Y researchers then published a book about *Ambiguous Evangelism*[18] suggesting ways to approach people who had little if any knowledge of the Christian faith and no overt spiritual appetite. The point I make here is simply that for most people, shaped by consumerist post-Christian culture, the journey to Christian faith and worship can be a long one. Paul Moore, vicar of the original Messy Church, warns practitioners to 'allow for the long journey people go on as they come from initial interest to openness to respond to the gospel'.[19]

The Generation Y researchers distinguished between 'formative' and 'transformative' spirituality.[20] 'Formative' spirituality 'is inherent in the human condition' and evidenced through 'awe, delight, meaning making, value making' and so on but 'may not be recognized by the individual as spiritual'. Ann Morisy similarly contrasted 'the foundational domain' with the 'explicit domain'.[21] The missional call is to enable people to move beyond the formative and foundational to the explicit transformative spirituality of Christian worship.

Missional liturgy/sacramental mission

If the sacraments are to be operative as doors to the sacred for previously unchurched people then the Church must lay, or clear, pathways to these doors. Fresh expressions normally[22] begin with a process of listening and community engagement, rather than with the immediate establishment of a new worship service.[23] This is because Christian mission is an incarnational ministry, which enters the everyday context of those it seeks to win. It is a ministry of grace. Grace meets people where they are, although it does not leave them there. This process makes it much more likely that the proposed new congregation will become a culturally appropriate community of disciples, rather than just a new worship event. If people with no church background are to become worshipping disciples then the process of listening and engagement might well include appropriate 'ritual' or liturgical events.

Ritual and 'liturgy' are still an everyday part of life beyond the Church. Sociologists who study the public's use of digital media use ritual as a category to make sense of our social media habits.[24] 'The secular nature of media does not prevent media generating ritual.'[25] Elsewhere in society the placing or flowers at the site of an accident or tragedy has become a customary ritual act, as has the candlelit vigil. We use ritual to express what words alone cannot communicate, or to connect major events of our lives to some sense of meaning. Pioneers, or teams, planting fresh expressions need to make simple appropriate ritual part of their missional practice; developing what Ann Morisy calls 'apt liturgy'.[26] Helping people to make sense of the events of life, to mark significant anniversaries, beginnings and endings, or to express care and concern for their communities is a vital part of Christian presence and service. Apt liturgy in everyday life prepares people for apt liturgy in Christian worship. Simple sacramental acts, helping them to make sense of their experience of life, open up pathways towards the dominical sacraments.

Believing before belonging

The dominical sacraments are both boundary markers and invitations to participate. Baptism publicly identifies Christian disciples, and because it is public invites others to discipleship. The Eucharist is the family meal of the people of God, and a foretaste of God's kingdom, but it is also a public invitation to dine. It is vital that the celebration of these sacraments in fresh expressions maintains both these dimensions. The purpose being, to draw new disciples in, rather than create a 'members only' culture.

'Believing before belonging' is a vital part of the journey to faith of many non-churched people. A welcoming community enables them to participate in the Christian community's life, as the context of exploring the claims of the Christian faith. Healthy Fresh Expressions of Church will welcome all, but call each to a step nearer to Christ. They will be at ease with untidiness, and with different levels of commitment being present simultaneously. They will not pressure everyone to move on in faith at the same time, but invite each to respond to Christ's call when they are able. They will be centred sets rather than bounded sets. Their culture will be to draw their participants into a continuum of discipleship: to initial discipleship and then on to mature discipleship: always 'further in and further up'.[27] The aim is to have a deeply committed, numerically growing, core of missional disciples as the centre of the fresh expression, but to create this in such a way that it attracts and draws others in, without pressuring them to express levels of commitment or understanding for which they are not yet ready. Inclusive hospitality is the vital context for sacramental ministry.

If baptism is the sacrament of Christian initiation, the Eucharist is the waymarker of committed faith. It is the repeated act through which we renew our identity as Christians and refocus our lives of discipleship. It also has the capacity to be a 'converting ordinance', although decisions about who may or may not participate need careful thought. The downside of the proper theological identification of Holy Communion as the central act of Christian worship is that, in some traditions, it has been interpreted to mean that every 'main' service has to be a Communion service. Care needs to be taken that this does not make every service seem like a 'members only' service. A mixed diet of eucharistic and word-focused services may be best, when numbers of not yet Christians are regularly present. In such circumstances public worship functions, for some, as a key element of a catechumenate process.

Waymarkers

The community life of a fresh expression of church needs to include waymarkers, public opportunities for people to take a step nearer to Christian commitment, or deeper in their discipleship, as and when each is ready.[28] The Roman Catholic Church's Rite of Christian Initiation of Adults[29] is helpful here. It distinguishes between 'the Period of Evangelization' – when enquirers are beginning to clarify what they are seeking, the questions they are asking, and hear the gospel for the first time, from 'the Period of the Catechumenate' – where the focus is to learn what it means to follow Christ in his Church. There is no time limit on either of these stages. They last as long as each enquirer needs them to last. Candidates then prepare for baptism during Lent and are baptized and admitted to the Eucharist at Easter. This Roman Catholic sequence is helpful for churches from other traditions.

The first stage may well take place through informal conversation, through hospitality in homes, or discussion events in neutral venues. All are welcome to start attending the regular worship of the fresh expression at any time, but it is not a requirement, and would be a step too far for some people. The second stage could involve an Alpha, Pilgrim or Christianity Explored course, or something specifically created for this group of people. It is more likely to be a group process and should normally include an invitation to attend worship as part of the process of learning, without attendance implying anything more than enquiry. In more liturgical or new monastic fresh expressions entry into the second stage may be marked publicly and liturgically, as in the Roman Catholic process. Both stages can be arranged for children. Fresh expressions like Messy Church could plan them for whole family groups.

Baptism, confirmation, or the renewal of baptismal vows makes the public transition from being an enquirer to a disciple, from welcome guest to family member. Like the Eucharist, baptism has a dual reference. It is both baptism into Christ, his death and resurrection (Romans 6.3ff.), and into his body the Church (1 Corinthians 12.12ff.). But it must not appear to be like joining a club! The focus is on faith in Christ. We have the privilege of introducing people to Jesus. Faith in him makes a Christian and, as a consequence, all Christians belong together in the family of God. 'Baptism constitutes our true family.'[30] We are the body of Christ because, personally and collectively we are 'in Christ' Whenever sacraments of initiation are celebrated, they should be public, in the presence of the whole church, and they should be celebrations, occasions of great joy.

Participation in the Eucharist requires both an assurance of God's gracious invitation, and an appropriate level of self-examination (1 Corinthians 11.28). The dual language of the body of Christ links the work of atonement to the community created by the cross. Full participation would normally be for those who confess faith in Christ or for those who use participation in a particular Eucharist to make their step of committed faith.[31] It may be best to explain the meaning of the rite, repeat Christ's invitation to repentance and faith, but then let the congregation self-regulate as to who participates, particularly if local practice normally involves passing the elements to one another.

In the earliest Church the Eucharist was not a ritual detached from life. It was celebrated in the context of a meal. It was shared around 'the Lord's table'. Best practice in planting fresh expressions of church aims to establish a community of faith, not just an event for worship. Communities eat together, so it would be very appropriate to celebrate Holy Communion at a community meal, on special occasions at least. Restored to this New Testament context it more easily embodies the dual meaning of the body of Christ, his atoning death and the new community that death makes possible. But the inclusion of new believers into the eucharistic community makes demands on the existing congregation, whether relatively new itself or long established. The apostle Paul made very strong criticisms of the practice of the Eucharist in Corinth (1 Corinthians 11.17–22, 27–34). Their liturgy may have been perfect, but it was used to reinforce existing social divisions and 'humiliate those who have nothing', in doing so showing 'contempt for the church of God'. The feast of the body and blood of Christ was carried out in a way that totally undermined its purpose. Its participants ate and drank 'without discerning the body'.[32] Admission to the Eucharist is admission to a counter-cultural community which fully welcomes everyone whom Christ calls.[33]

'The Eucharist most fundamentally links hospitality with God.'[34]

Those who are shaped by Christ's eucharistic hospitality in this way are empowered to offer hospitality around their own tables at home: to be hosts who welcome friends, neighbours, strangers and those in need; and sometimes providing the setting for their acquaintances' first stages of enquiry (Luke 14.12–14). Equally, those who have first received Christ's hospitality in Holy Communion, now bear the good news to others, and are to be open to receive the hospitality offered to them; to be the guests not the hosts. 'Eating with "sinners" was one of the most characteristic and striking marks of Jesus' regular activity.'[35] One fresh expression in South Africa began when a church congregation chose to put on a meal one night per week when they would invite the local community and eat 'with' them. Large numbers of rough sleepers began to attend, because this was not a soup kitchen 'for' them, but acceptance of them as equals. The meals led to many conversations about faith. The conversations led to the meals concluding with an act of worship. We have much to learn from 'the meal habits of the Messiah'.[36] Like their Lord, missional disciples bring peace (Luke 10.5–7). In these ways pathways are cleared from the Lord's table to our neighbours' tables, and then back again.[37]

The establishment of sacramental life in fresh expressions of church dare not be treated as a late-stage development, which assumes that once new people get sufficiently used to church language, we can then stage a baptism or celebrate the Eucharist much as we would anywhere. The foundation of incarnational mission and inclusive hospitality must be laid. Pathways need to be patiently laid, which link everyday life outside the Church with the Church's sacraments. The gospel sacraments need to be performed contextually and, true to their nature, transformationally, to equip disciples for patient hospitable incarnational mission. It is time to open new doors for the gospel and lay new paths between the world and the Church.

Notes

1 Since this chapter was completed, a fuller research report, 'The Day of Small Things', has been published on 21 dioceses. It can be downloaded at www.churcharmy.org/Groups/244966/Church_Army/Church_Army/Our_work/Research/Fresh_expressions_of/Fresh_expressions_of.aspx.

2 Joseph Martos, *Doors to the Sacred*, SCM Press, Norwich, 1981.

3 See Christine Pohl, *Making Room: Recovering Hospitality as a Christian Tradition*, Eerdmans, Grand Rapids, 1999.

4 E.g. by using the 'Everybody Welcome' course by Bob Jackson and George Fisher.

5 *Fresh Expressions in the Mission of the Church*, Church House Publishing, London, 2012, p. 188, defines 'locality' as 'a context which is neither exclusively territorial, nor purely associational but relational, and therefore inclusive of both'.

6 E.g. see *Eucharistic Presidency*, Church House Publishing, London, 1997.

7 The York Statement 'Down to Earth Worship' in *Liturgical Inculturation in the Anglican Communion*, ed. David R. Holeton, Grove Books, Nottingham, 1990, p. 6.

8 See Steve Aisthorpe, *The Invisible Church*, St Andrew Press, Edinburgh, 2016.

9 Tearfund data plus under 16s.

10 As encouraged for Back to Church Sunday.

11 Christopher Lasch, *The Culture of Narcissism*, Norton, New York, 1979, p. 7.

12 Mark Berry, 'Engagement with Spiritual Seekers in New Monasticism as Fresh Expression of Church', in Graham Cray, Ian Mobsby and Aaron Kennedy (eds), *New Monasticism as Fresh Expression of Church*, Canterbury Press, Norwich, 2010, pp. 59–60.

13 See Graham Cray, *Disciples and Citizens*, Inter-Varsity Press, Nottingham, 2007, pp. 73–7.

14 Sara Savage, Sylvia Collins-Mayo, Bob Mayo, Graham Cray, *Making Sense of Generation Y: The World View of 15- to 25-year-olds*, Church House Publishing, London, 2006.

15 Savage et al., *Making Sense of Generation Y*, p. 37.

16 Savage et al., *Making Sense of Generation Y*, p. 23.

17 Graham Cray, 'The Eucharist and the Postmodern World', in Pete Ward (ed.), *Mass Culture*, Bible Reading Fellowship, Abingdon, 2008.

18 Bob Mayo with Sara Savage and Sylvie Collins, *Ambiguous Evangelism*, SPCK, London, 2004.

19 Paul Moore, in Graham Cray, *Making Disciples in Fresh Expressions of Church*, Share Booklet, Fresh Expressions, www.freshexpressions.org.uk, 2013, p. 11.

20 Savage et al., *Making Sense of Generation Y*, pp. 12ff.

21 Ann Morisy, *Journeying Out: A New Approach to Christian Mission*, Morehouse, New York, 2004, chapters 7 and 8.

22 There are notable exceptions to this general principle, as in Father Damian's Feeney's weekly eucharist at East Preston ASDA.

23 See Michael Moynagh, *Church for Every Context*, SCM Press, Norwich, 2012, pp. 205–10.

24 E.g. Nick Couldry, *Media Rituals: A Critical Approach*, Routledge, London and New York, 2003; and *Media, Society, World: Social Theory and Digital Media Practice*, Polity Press, Cambridge, 2012.

25 Couldry, *Media, Society, World*, p. 71.

26 Morisy, *Journeying Out*, pp. 156–71.

27 As in C. S. Lewis, *The Last Battle*, Harper Collins, London, 2009.

28 For two examples, Moot and Sorted, see Cray *Making Disciples in Fresh Expressions of Church*, pp. 24ff.

29 http://www.rcia.org.uk/resources/10-principles-of-rcia/.

30 Stanley Hauerwas, 'The Liturgical Shape of the Christian Life', in David Ford and Dennis Stamps, *Essentials of Christian Community*, T&T Clark, 1996, p. 44.

31 The rubric in the Book of Common Prayer identifies Holy Communion as being for those confirmed, or 'desirous of being confirmed'. The latter gives Anglicans some leeway.

32 For more on this see George Hunsinger, *The Eucharist and Ecumenism*, Cambridge University Press, Cambridge, 2008, pp. 252–63.

33 For Paul's inversion of the standard Graeco-Roman use of the 'body' metaphor see David Horrell, *Solidarity and Difference*, T&T Clark, London, 2005, pp. 122–4.

34 Christine Pohl, *Making Room: Recovering Hospitality as a Christian Tradition*, Eerdmans, Grand Rapids, 1999, p. 30.

35 N. T. Wright, *Jesus and the Victory of God*, SPCK, London 1996, p. 431.

36 See Conrad Gempf, *The Mealtime Habits of the Messiah*, Zondervan, Grand Rapids, 2006.

37 I acknowledge David Fitch as the source of this understanding of the missional reach of the Eucharist. For a full elaboration see his *Faithful Presence*, Inter-Varsity Press, London, chapter 3, 2016.

2

The Glory of God in Everyday Life: Culture, Spirituality and Sacrament

JOHN DRANE

Douglas Coupland is a Canadian artist and writer who has a reputation as an insightful commentator on the changing shape of contemporary culture and the challenges that we face in attempting to navigate a safe passage through the fast-moving currents and cross-currents of everyday life. His first novel popularized 'Generation X' as a description of those who were born between the early 1960s and mid-1970s,[1] and all his subsequent writings have inspired reflection on the meaning of life and relationships in the context of a world that is changing at breakneck speed in ways that are discontinuous with the past and unpredictable in their outcome. One of his more provocative books is *Life after God*, which in its original hardback version was designed to sit comfortably in the hand, and with the shape of a hand embossed into the front cover as if to offer a supportive presence to readers as they ponder the questions of meaning and purpose facing those who, as the dust jacket proclaims, are only too well aware that 'You are the first generation raised without religion'. The text on the jacket continues by asking:

> What happens if we are raised without religion or beliefs? As we grow older, the beauty and disenchantments of the world temper our souls. We are all living creatures with strong religious impulses, yet where do these impulses flow in a world of malls and TV, Kraft dinner and jets?

Almost 300 pages later, he writes: 'I must remind myself we are living creatures – we have religious impulses – we *must* – and yet into what cracks do these impulses flow in a world without religion? It is something I think about every day. Sometimes I think it is the only thing I should be thinking about.'[2] And by the penultimate last page he arrives at this conclusion:

> Now – here is my secret: I tell it to you with an openness of heart that I doubt I shall ever achieve again, so I pray that you are in a quiet room as you hear these words. My secret is that I need God – that I am sick and can no longer make it alone. I need God to help me give, because I no longer seem to be capable of giving; to help me be kind, as I no longer seem capable of kindness; to help me love, as I seem beyond being able to love.[3]

While it would be an exaggeration to suggest that everyone is reflecting on these questions with the same intensity as the characters in a Coupland novel, the matters to which he draws attention are a recurring theme for very many people, revolving as they do around transient relationships, misleading advertising, post-truth politics and environmental upheaval, not to mention the sheer boredom and drudgery that characterizes many workplaces. This scenario is nothing new: centuries ago the writer of Ecclesiastes complained that while we seem to have an inbuilt aspiration for life to be full of meaning and purpose, in reality 'everything was vanity, a chasing after the wind' (2.11) – a chasing that for him involved a search for deeper experiences through intoxication, food, consumerism, sex, music and more. It is no coincidence that my colleague at Fuller Seminary, Robert Johnston, was able to write a commentary on Ecclesiastes that is entirely illustrated through reference to Hollywood movies,[4] because Douglas Coupland is by no means alone in wrestling with this uncomfortable space in which life can seem more or less meaningless and yet there persists a feeling that, if only we can find the key, there must be some experience that – however fleeting – can offer transformation of the dull moments, if not a complete resolution of our individual angst and corporate nihilism.

Searching for meaning

We do not need to look far to find evidence of the search for transformational encounters. There has probably never been a generation more saturated in experiences, whether it is through immersion in the world of video games[5] or what might look to be the more mundane but equally obsessive need that most of us have to be constantly looking into our phones in the elusive search for something – anything – that will connect us with a bigger reality beyond ourselves and assure us that the value of our otherwise insignificant existence has recognition somewhere, if only because others retweet our opinions.[6] Beyond that though, a growing army of people engage in a more self-conscious search for experiences that will lift us out of the moment and into some other level of consciousness. For some that will be experimentation with sex or drugs, while for many more it will be following a favourite sports team, and for yet others it will be some sort of engagement with the natural world whether through the relative safety of mountaineering or the less predictable thrill represented by extreme sports such as tombstoning or cage diving with deadly sharks. There has also been a revolution on our high streets, as everyday therapies are repackaged as immersive experiences that can offer more than merely physical benefits. While I was writing this chapter, an Australian friend received an invitation from a therapist specializing in 'Archangel Aromatherapy', which offers the opportunity to 'Experience these divine oils and learn which Archangel will help you heal, transform and create your identity'.[7] People have known for centuries that massage has health-giving properties, but now it is promoted not only as a way of reinvigorating tired muscles but as an experience that will change everything. The commodification of experiences has become one of the key growth industries of the twenty-first century.[8]

It is easy to be cynical about all this and see it as just another evidence of the trivialization and commercialization of life highlighted a generation ago by Neil Postman, whose bestselling title said it all: *Amusing Ourselves to Death*.[9] At the benign end of the spectrum are restaurants that offer to transport you into another world along with your meal. The primary appeal of the Hard Rock Café is not the food but the fact that you are surrounded by the sights, sounds and memorabilia of the music industry. Similarly, when diners at the Bubba Gump Shrimp Co flip the card saying 'Run Forrest, run', they are not just ordering an item of food or drink: you and the server are both living within a scene from the 1994 movie *Forrest Gump*. The meal is obviously important, but its unique selling point is the 'eatertainment' that is an essential part of the whole experience. After dining, you might go next door to a Hollister store whose design is supposed to evoke images of surfing on a Pacific beach, and where you become part of an entirely fictional story of one John Hollister, who is said to have established it in 1922 following a trip to the Dutch East Indies. The truth is more mundane (it was established in 2000 by the upmarket clothing company Abercrombie and Fitch), but that is not a problem in a world where a visit to a Disney theme park can take you in quick succession from a Parisian boulevard to a scene from the jungle, a fairy castle, or Main Street from a hundred years ago. Churches have even got in on the act. It is now possible to spend a day in a full-size replica of Noah's ark, meet his family, see the animals they deposited on Mt Ararat, and discover 'biblical fossils'.[10] At the Holy Land Experience you can meet priests going about their duties in the ancient Jerusalem temple, watch Jesus perform miracles, or walk the streets of gold in the new creation. You could even be born again, baptized by John the Baptist, and relive the Day of Pentecost.[11]

It is easy to be cynical about some of this, but the desire for an encounter that will take you into some alien environment appears to be built into the human psyche. If it can also provide a little excitement, then so much the better. Traditional funfairs have always offered the thrill of being terrified, whether on a roller coaster or ghost train, though with the expectation that all will be well – and when something goes wrong we complain and sue the operators. The lyrics of many traditional hymns (not to mention the Psalms of the Old Testament) frequently reflect a similar pattern of alienation and fear, which then gives way to deliverance.[12] Far from diminishing this need, the health and safety culture with which we now cocoon ourselves has created its own impetus for us to indulge in artificially created experiences of fear and its resolution. The commercialization of experience cannot be denied, but that is not the only motivation for seeking experiences that will, however momentarily, transcend everyday life. Many such experiences are far removed from the artificial world of the theme park, and while mountaineering or skydiving might be commercially organized, the main attraction offered by such activities is their connection to the world of nature with its unpredictability and potential for disaster.

Experiencing the spiritual

Snowboarding is one example of an immersive experience that has been researched in relation to its spiritual dimension by Neil Elliot, a Church of England priest now living in Canada who gained a PhD from a British university on the basis of his research into the subject.[13] He discovered that boarders often describe their sport as 'soul riding', which is typically described in the following terms:

> Sometimes it all seems to go silent, and it's just you and the snow. Even the sensation of constant turning disappears. At these moments, you are both completely focused on your riding, aware of every nuance of the snow and your board, and almost detached, as if the board is guiding itself and you are just a passenger. Time stops.[14]

Though I am hopeless at snowboarding, I have no difficulty in identifying with that and I can recall at least two occasions when I had a comparable experience while skiing. One was at the end of a spring day on the slopes at Glen Coe in Scotland, when almost everyone else had left and (somewhat unusually for a Scottish ski centre) the snow was deep and the sun was spilling an orange glow over it as I and my companions were on our final run of the day. The other was not long after dawn in Whistler (Canada) when I had ascended the mountain in the darkness and was one of the first skiers to come down on that morning. When we reached the bottom, my wife Olive commented that this must be what God felt like on the day of creation – and I knew exactly what she meant, because she put into words what I was feeling myself, and when I came across Neil Elliot's description I immediately identified it as the same sort of experience.

Richard and Lorimer Passmore have observed a similar phenomenon as detached youth workers with skaters.[15] The young people they met spoke intuitively of their experience in performing jumps as an encounter with 'the Flow' – terminology around which they developed an indigenous theology and which naturally invites comparison with the work of psychology professor Mihály Csíkszentmihályi, who used the same word to describe that immersive state of consciousness which others might refer to as being 'in the groove' or 'in the zone', and which is familiar to many musicians and artists as well as sports people.[16] None of this is unique to people in the twenty-first century of course, and one can reasonably assume that mystics through the centuries refer to similar experiences of ecstasy and connection to some ultimate reality.

There are significant missional connections to be made with historic understandings of the sacramental, though in order to make them we will need an expansive understanding of the *missio Dei* and a more radical understanding of the nature of sacrament, on which there is an extensive literature – much of it relating to issues that have more to do with power politics than with theology. The origin of the word itself is fairly uncontroversial, and can be traced to the Latin words *sacrum momentum* ('a sacred moment'), which subsequently came to be associated with *sacramentum*, another Latin word that meant something slightly different. Equally uncontroversial is the fact that, since the New Testament was written in Greek and not Latin, the word itself is never found in the original form of Scripture but was chosen as a Latin equivalent of the Greek word *mysterion*, meaning 'mystery'. In antiquity, a 'mystery' was not something puzzling, but referred to that transcendent quality of human life that could most readily be recognized as a connection with the divine. The many 'mystery religions' of the Roman Empire provided the most tangible expression of this, with their intention of enabling initiates to connect with the timeless realities of the cosmos through participation in ritual experiences by means of which it was believed one could be enlightened. Plato provided the underlying world view for this with his distinction between the material world and the 'real' or 'ideal' world, and Augustine's influential notion that sacraments are visible signs of an invisible reality was a perfect expression of Platonic thinking.[17] By his time, though, there had been two other significant developments. On the one hand, the usefulness of the concept of 'mystery' as a way of contextualizing the gospel meant that Christianity was often being presented as a form of mystery religion in which (building on Paul's themes in Romans 6 and 1 Corinthians 10.17) baptism and Eucharist came to be regarded as a mystical participation in the death and resurrection of Christ. Alongside this, Tertullian had adapted the civic significance of the word *sacramentum*, meaning the taking of an oath as a voluntary act of commitment – something that also had resonances with the initiation rites of the mystery religions, in which a person would typically take an oath of commitment to the group and its secrets. In the context of the Church's practices, this connection introduced an ambivalence between an emphasis on God's freely given grace and the believer's response as an act of commitment – a tension that continues to define the sacramental understandings and practice of different denominations even today.

An awareness of this historical background not only serves to highlight the importance of defining our terms, but can also offer some clues as to how we might connect the biblical tradition in particular with the search for meaning and purpose of people in the twenty-first century. The use of the term *mysterion* is well illustrated in The Wisdom of Solomon, where we find two separate, though related, implications of the word: on the one hand it is a way of referring to 'the purposes (or plan) of God' (2.22), while on the other it can refer to 'knowledge of God' (8.4). This is not rational knowledge of propositions and theories, but the sort of knowledge that Adam and Eve had of one another when they engaged in sexual intimacies – in other words, knowledge as activity and experience.[18] This usage continues in the New Testament, most obviously in the writings of Paul, where *mysterion* is embodied in Christ (Colossians 2.2), revealed by the work of the Spirit (1 Corinthians 2.10–15), and is experienced, among other things, as reconciliation between different people groups (Ephesians 3.2–6). Moreover, this is a pattern that, while the specific details may differ, recurs throughout Scripture. Typical examples of such encounters would include Jacob's angelic encounters (Genesis 28.10–22; 32.22–32), Moses at the burning bush (Exodus 3.1–6), Elijah's experience of the earthquake, fire, and still small voice (1 Kings 19.11–13), and Amos's vision of locusts (Amos 7.1–6), plumbline (7.7–9) and summer fruits (8.1–3), or Job's encounter with a whirlwind that introduced him to God's presence in the forces of nature (Job 38.1–7). Then there is Isaiah's experience of God's call as he participated in worship (Isaiah 6.1–8). Expositions of that story have often focused on the content of the message that Isaiah was given to convey to his people, but the medium through which the message came to the prophet engaged all his senses as he was caught up in an encounter with heavenly messengers and the voice of God. Then there are the stories of Ezekiel's extraordinary experiences of being transported into what can only be described as a parallel universe (Ezekiel 1.4–28; 8.1—11.25 etc.) – experiences that the prophet seems to have sought with some intentionality, perhaps paralleling the way that in more recent times some have argued for a connection between drugs and the search for spiritual experience.[19] Ezekiel's use of such mind-altering substances may be debateable, but there can be no doubt that some biblical prophets utilized music and dance as a way of inducing the sort of oceanic experiences in which transcendent connections are made with a reality that is greater than and beyond themselves (1 Samuel 10.5–6; 19.20–24).[20]

Challenges for the Church

In the past, one of the attractions that church held for people was to lift them out of the tediousness and sheer boredom of everyday life. The drama of worship offered an immersive theatrical experience in which transcendent realities could transform the human soul through all the senses of touch, taste, sight, smell and sound, in ways not unlike Isaiah's temple experience. I have previously written at some length about our collusion with the forces of rationalization in relation to both mission and worship.[21] For some traditions that was intentional, and not only was worship reduced to an essentially cognitive activity but even health-giving activities like sport and physical exercise came to be regarded as a sinful distraction from the serious business of safeguarding one's eternal destiny.[22] For many other traditions, however, the slide into such ways of being has been more accidental, perhaps driven by an over-reliance on the Cartesian dictum that 'I think, therefore I am' and reinforced by a cultural trend that embraced order and discipline while never getting too excited about anything – in other words, the McDonaldized church of efficiency, predictability, calculability and control. It can be argued that in some cultures this rationalized way of being church might be an appropriate contextualization of the faith, but that is certainly not true of Western nations today, where we are living in a sort of cultural limbo, with over-rationalized structures still dominating many aspects of civic and commercial life at the same time as people are looking for meaning by embracing attitudes that are less prescriptive and at times anarchic. Is this the point at which we can begin to make connections between the mystery of which the Bible speaks and the search for transcendence through something – anything – that looks as if it might add colour and excitement to our otherwise dull lives?

At the beginning of the twenty-first century David Hay and Kate Hunt published their research on what they called 'the spirituality of people who don't go to church', in which they reflected on case studies of people whose reported experiences were not so very different from those we have mentioned so far. Some of them were entirely unsought, much like the stories of Moses or Paul in the Bible, while others were the result of an intentional searching.[23] Hay's lifelong research was devoted to exploring whether our sense of the spiritual might in some way be biologically determined,[24] but regardless of our opinion on that, in missional terms the question to ask is not 'How can we make people spiritual?' (because they already are), but rather 'How does that innate spirituality relate to an experience of God in Christ?' Augustine listed more than three hundred things that he regarded as sacraments, and while they included distinctively ecclesiastical rituals such as baptism, Eucharist, penance and chrism, he also listed things like contemplation, bowing one's head, taking off one's shoes, music and singing, along with reconciliation and other social actions as authentic expressions of divine realities. Many of these were by no means unique to Christians, which suggests that Augustine approached the subject from what today we might call a missional perspective, recognizing that God could be encountered through them even when Christian faith was not overtly named.[25] If so, then he and others like him were building on the approach documented by Luke in his account of Paul's visit to Athens (Acts 17.16–34), where devotion to the 'unknown god' – something with no obvious Judeo-Christian connection – was understood not as something alien but as a pointer to Christ. Of course, as Paul went on to explain, that was not the whole story, but the underlying assumption was that the extant spiritual experience of the Athenians was not in conflict with the gospel, but was a foundational staging post in a genuine encounter with God in Christ.

This poses a question for us: how might we affirm the value of the self-defined spirituality of our own contemporaries as part of an authentic journey towards God as revealed in Jesus Christ? In his study of the spirituality of snowboarding,

Neil Elliot identified three interrelated themes: the experiences in and of themselves, the context, and then what might really be going on in terms of personhood and an individual's sense of belonging in the greater scheme of things. In relation to the actual experiences, then if God is active in the world (the *missio Dei*), it should not be too difficult to acknowledge the authenticity of what people report because we can expect that, as Jesus said, those who are honestly seeking spiritual reality will find it (Matthew 7.7); and on the ultimate question of what is actually going on in the deepest recesses of someone's person, we can leave that to God while recognizing the importance of discernment on our part. Context is a point where we ought to be able to make appropriate connections, though that means that this discussion will inevitably end with more questions than answers because culture is now so fractured and fragmented that we can no longer speak of 'culture' (and therefore context) in a specific sense but only of 'cultures' (and therefore of contexts, plural). We can, however, identify some of the challenges with which we must grapple. One of them has been well expressed by Craig Detweiler and Barry Taylor, who in light of their analysis of broader cultural trends conclude that 'sacramental churches are poised for a comeback'.[26] That might sound like good news, but the sting in the tail is their proposal:

> It is time to take the consecrated bread out of the tabernacle and place it in the hands of ordinary people, offering them a new portrait of holiness. Popular culture continues to redefine the relationship between the sacred and the secular, the holy and the profane. People of faith should do the same.[27]

Another challenge is that posed by Joseph Pine and James Gilmore (who are both Christians and write with some insight into the situation of the Church). In commenting on the tendency of some people to go from one experience to another in the search for one that somehow 'works', they argue that what people are looking for is not experience per se, but transformation, and in order to facilitate that we 'must learn to stage a rich, compelling experience.'[28] That, of course, is what we would like to think we are doing in our worship. But they also warn that those who focus only on the provision of experiences

> without considering the effect these experiences will have on the participants and without designing the experiences in such a way as to create a desired change – will eventually see their experiences become commoditized. The second time you experience something, it will be marginally less enjoyable than the first time, the third time less enjoyable than that, and so on until you finally notice the experience doesn't engage you nearly as much as it once did. Welcome to the commoditization of experiences, best exemplified by the increasingly voiced phrase, 'Been there, done that.' . . . When you customize an experience, you automatically turn it into a *transformation* . . .[29]

In our context, moving from experience to transformation implies discipleship – but that is something that would require a whole chapter to itself.

Notes

1 Douglas Coupland, *Generation X: Tales for an Accelerated Culture*, St Martin's Press, New York, 1991.

2 Douglas Coupland, *Life after God*, Simon & Schuster, London, 1994, p. 273.

3 Coupland, *Life after God*, p. 359.

4 Robert K. Johnston, *Useless Beauty: Ecclesiastes through the Lens of Contemporary Film*, Baker Academic, Grand Rapids, 2004.

5 On the spirituality of gaming, see Craig Detweiler (ed.), *Halos and Avatars: Playing Video Games with God*, Westminster John Knox Press, Louisville, 2010.

6 Craig Detweiler, *iGods: How Technology Shapes Our Spiritual and Social Lives*, Brazos Press, Grand Rapids, 2013.

7 www.rachaelwhite.com.au/ – accessed November 2016. For in-depth discussion of such topics, see Ross Clifford and Philip Johnson, *Taboo or To Do: Is Christianity Complementary with Yoga, Martial Arts, Hallowe'en, Mindfulness and other Alternative Practices?*, Darton, Longman & Todd, London, 2016.

8 B. Joseph Pine and James H. Gilmore, *The Experience Economy*, Harvard Business School Press, Boston, 1999.

9 Neil Postman, *Amusing Ourselves to Death: Public Discourse in the Age of Show Business*, Penguin, New York, 1985.

10 www.arkencounter.com – accessed November 2016.

11 www.holylandexperience.com – accessed November 2016.

12 John Newton's 'Amazing Grace' is an example of one that is known and loved well beyond religious circles: I wonder to what extent the pattern of fear followed by deliverance contributes to that popularity?

13 Neil R. M. Elliot, '"Soulriding" and the Spirituality of Snowboarding', PhD thesis, Kingston University, London, 2010. For a brief overview, see www.kingston.ac.uk/news/article/325/30-mar-2011-spirituality-on-the-slopes-vicar-gains-phd-in-snowboarding/ – accessed November 2016.

14 www.anglicanjournal.com/articles/soul-rider-10349 – accessed November 2016.

15 Richard and Lorimer Passmore, *Here be Dragons: Youth Work and Mission off the Map*, Frontier Youth Trust, Birmingham, 2013.

16 For a classic exposition of the theme see Mihály Csíkszentmihályi, *Flow: The Psychology of Happiness*, Rider, London, 2002.

17 'One thing is seen while another is grasped; what is seen is a physical likeness, what is grasped bears spiritual fruit' (Augustine, *Sermon* 272).

18 'Adam knew Eve . . . and she conceived' (Genesis 4.1, KJV).

19 Alexander Shulgin and Ann Shulgin, *TIHKAL: The Continuation*, Transform Press, Berkeley, 1997; Timothy Leary, *The Politics of Ecstasy*, 4th edn, Ronin Publishing, Berkeley, 1998.

20 Simon Reynolds, *Energy Flash: A Journey through Rave Music and Dance Culture*, Picador, London, 1998; Ben Malbon, *Clubbing: Dancing, Ecstasy and Vitality*, Routledge, London, 1999; Nicholas Saunders et al., *In Search of the Ultimate High*, Rider, London, 2000; John Drane, 'Contemporary Culture and the Reinvention of Sacramental Spirituality', in Geoffrey Rowell and Christine Hall (eds), *The Gestures of God*, Continuum, London, 2004, pp. 37–55.

21 John Drane, *The McDonaldization of the Church*, Darton Longman & Todd, London, 2000; *After McDonaldization*, Darton Longman & Todd, London, 2008.

22 Lincoln Harvey, *A Brief Theology of Sport*, SCM Press, London, 2014, pp. 49–56.

23 David Hay and Kate Hunt, *Understanding the Spirituality of People Who don't go to Church*, University of Nottingham School of Education, Nottingham, 2000.

24 David Hay, *Something There: The Biology of the Human Spirit*, Darton, Longman & Todd, London, 2006; *Why Spirituality is Difficult for Westerners*, Societas Imprint Academic, Exeter, 2007.

25 C. S. Lewis concluded that, for very similar reasons, the practices of early medieval pagans and Christians were often difficult to distinguish: see his *The Discarded Image*, Cambridge University Press, Cambridge, 1964.

26 Craig Detweiler and Barry Taylor, *A Matrix of Meanings: Finding God in Pop Culture*, Baker Academic, Grand Rapids, 2003, p. 301.

27 Detweiler and Taylor, *A Matrix of Meanings*, p. 291.

28 Pine and Gilmore, *The Experience Economy*, p. 25.

29 Pine and Gilmore, *The Experience Economy*, p. 165; emphasis in original.

3

Made in the Image of God: Encountering the Creator through Creativity

OLIVE FLEMING DRANE

Andrew M. Greeley was a Roman Catholic priest and sociologist, and almost 30 years ago he wrote these words which neatly summarize the sort of questions that I want to reflect on in this chapter:

> If one believes that people are sacraments of God, that God discloses himself/herself to us through objects, events, and persons of life, then one must concede the possibility that in the sacramentality of ordinary folk, their hopes, their fears, their loves, their aspirations represent a legitimate experience of God, legitimate symbols of God, and legitimate stories of God.[1]

In the light of later Christian history, that may seem to be a provocative claim, but in reality it is only expressing what is already stated clearly enough on the very first page of the Bible. In the creation hymn of Genesis 1, there are two key themes: the first is that God is the origin of everything that is, and God's very being is manifested in the creativity and imagination that we see around us in the physicality of the world; and the second is that people are made 'in the image of God' (Genesis 1.27). Many complex understandings of the *imago Dei* have been proposed over the centuries, but in this original context its meaning is simple: we most authentically reflect that God-given identity when we ourselves display the same creative imagination that is to be found at the heart of all things. In order to unpack some of the consequences of that, I want to begin by sharing some stories and then to reflect on the questions that we might now need to address in a missional context.

Spirituality in the workplace

Recent years have seen a growing recognition of things 'spiritual' among public bodies, and all the caring professions are now expected (in some cases legally required) to have due regard for the spiritual well-being of their clients. When I was invited to lead a workshop on spiritual care for the social work department in one of our Scottish cities, I naturally gave a good deal of thought as to what this might entail, and my starting point was a feeling that in order to do this effectively for others, social workers would need to address their own spirituality. As we gathered I placed a large block of ice in the centre of the group, and suggested that this might be the way many people have experienced the spiritual – as something cold, inaccessible and unattractive. After introductions we got to work making dough, which each person used to create a symbol that would reflect their own spiritual self-understanding. After the dough symbols went off to prove and then be baked in the oven, we made collages, drew life graphs and talked about the perceived spiritual needs of typical social work clients. Throughout the day, the frozen block silently observed all our conversations, and inevitably gradually melted so that by the time we got to the final session of the day it was mostly liquid. To wrap things up, I invited each person to take their bread symbol and share it with everyone else, tearing off a piece and telling each one what they had most appreciated about the contribution they had made that day. Though it was not my original intention, it was not long before someone suggested they might share the liquid that had oozed from the ice. What I had not told them up to this point was that the block of ice was not pure frozen water, but had red wine mixed in with it – something that was by now obvious anyway from its colour. One or two commented about this being just like the last supper of Jesus – and then the really interesting conversations began, as others reminisced about their own lost or forgotten Christian roots and what it might now mean were they to rediscover them. The theme continued in the course evaluations, with many expressing surprise that a course in professional development could also be spiritually enriching. In one of his sermons on the Eucharist, Augustine commented that 'one thing is seen while another is grasped; what is seen is a physical likeness, what is grasped bears spiritual fruit'[2] – so on that understanding, did at least some of the participants have a sacramental experience? We will come back to that, but first some more stories.

Missional creativity

Mention of Jesus' last supper highlights the importance of food in creating the sort of community that is at the heart of many Fresh Expressions of Church. At the time I first met them, *Fridays in Faith* was an ecumenical monthly event for all ages in Annan, a small town in south-west Scotland not far from Carlisle. After many successful gatherings, the leaders decided to include a sharing of broken bread as a reflective focus for all those attending. Four loaves were placed on a central table and the episode was distinguished from the rest of the evening by being designated as 'The Gathering'. The way the leaders described it in their introduction is a striking example of cultural creativity as well as theological depth and missional perception:

> We have been thinking of a way of sharing the hope that comes through God's brokenness.
>
> We would like to break this bread and share it together.
>
> Brokenness/sharing . . .
>
> The cross says, 'I am here for you' . . . This is for each of us here tonight.
>
> This is a simple act, open to every one of us. All are welcome . . .

Wherever you feel you are on your faith journey.

You can bring your doubts and fears . . . the good and the rubbish.

We don't understand how the seed becomes the flower . . .

We don't understand all that went on at the cross, but . . .

We can come and share this broken bread as a very simple sign of hope.

. . .

The only way we can share this bread is to break it: By the breaking of bread we are assured that in our brokenness there is hope.

This was not regarded as any sort of Eucharist, but reflected the theme for that evening which was *Gaze and Wonder* – a way of discovering the Easter message that would be equally accessible to all ages. Images of brokenness had already inspired conversations around the theme, and many participants found it to be a healing moment as they shared the bread and assured one another that there is indeed hope beyond brokenness.[3] If, as James F. White puts it, a sacrament is an encounter in which 'the outward can convey the inward and spiritual' in such a way that physical actions become a meeting place with the transcendent, in what sense was this a sacramental moment for those involved?[4]

The holy fool

I was once invited to take part as one of my clown characters in the closing service of a national urban mission conference. This was Barni, a hobo clown, and the invitation was for me to celebrate Barni's Feast in which the hobo sorts through her bag of items rescued from the street, which include stale bread, the remains of a bottle of wine, barbed wire, nails, a few cloths, a well-used candle and other odds and ends. In mime (no words spoken), I set all these things up as if on an altar, with actions that clearly reflect the last supper, and often then beckon others to share the bread and wine if they wish. As this was an ecumenical event, the organizers had asked me to partake of bread and wine myself but not invite others to join in. I had many qualms about this, but went along with it and did exactly as had been agreed, celebrating myself but leaving the loaf and the bottle on the altar and then departing as I had arrived, as one of the outcasts with my sweeping brush collecting anything that looked as if it might be useful. I could hardly believe what happened next. One of the key organizers of the whole event jumped up and announced that he was not prepared to leave until he had shared in Barni's Feast. So I was called back to the altar, whereupon everyone (including two bishops, one RC and the other Anglican) left their seats and pressed forward to be a part of the sharing of the bread and wine. If this had been in the plan, I would have had a beer mug chalice in my bag but because I was to be the only one who would eat or drink I left that out and, in typical hobo style, drank straight from the bottle, which meant that everyone else did likewise.[5] At the lunch which followed, it was obvious that this had become a very special moment of grace for all those who were present. So if, as John Wesley said, sacraments are 'a means of grace',[6] was this experience sacramental – and how did the creativity of clowning facilitate that?

Water

Water has a universal connection to spirituality.[7] Moreover, it provides the parenthesis within which the entire drama of the Bible takes place as the waters of chaos on the first page of Genesis (1.2) are transformed to become the water of the river of life on the last page of Revelation (22.1–6). In between are many stories in which water is the medium of deliverance, cleansing, healing, nurture and new life. It courses like a tidal wave through Scripture and played a prominent part in some of the festivals, most notably in the time of Jesus at the Feast of Tabernacles, which celebrated the gathering of the harvest.[8] So when I was invited to lead the harvest thanksgiving service at Fuller Seminary in Pasadena, I knew that we could do something creatively different while also being very true to our biblical heritage by using water, which of course has been in short supply in southern California for some time. As they arrived, everyone received a small bottle of water that we used in different ways throughout the service, taking an occasional sip to celebrate our unity with one another, our connection to the earth, and so on. Then as the final benediction, we had bowls around the place into which we all poured what we had left and where worshippers could choose to use it in whatever way was meaningful to them.

Some marked their friends with the sign of the cross, others washed their own or someone else's hands, while others took yet more to drink. One woman came to me and asked for her bottle of water to be poured over her so she would be soaked from head to foot. For a moment I wondered if she was serious. But she explained that she was a victim and survivor of abuse and had suddenly experienced this overwhelming sense of needing to be cleansed, and for it to happen there and then so that what she knew and wished for in her head could be made real through this ritual. That woman would previously have attended many harvest thanksgiving services, but on this occasion she found new life through a creative use of water – actually, more creative than I had ever envisaged, for I never imagined anyone would ask to be drenched in it! So what was going on? Was this a form of chrism for her, or an echo of baptism, which itself reflects the watery deluge through which we all came into the world and which became an image of new birth in Jesus' conversation with Nicodemus? (John 3.5).

What do these stones (stories) mean?[9]

With more space I could add many other examples of creative imagination leading to profound encounters with the divine: stories of film, colouring books, icons, cooking, sport, dance . . . the list is endless, which should not surprise us if it is indeed true that, in the words of Joan Osborne's famous song, 'God was one of us'. But it is now time to enquire more specifically about what is going on here, and how any of it connects with what the Church traditionally understands as a sacrament. And that takes us into another aspect of creativity that is experiencing a significant revival today: storytelling.

A hundred years ago, one of the topics occupying what was then cutting-edge biblical scholarship was the relationship between myth and ritual. New understandings of religious traditions from the practices of ancient Babylon to the folklore of Nordic lands raised the question of how what we say (myth) correlates with what we do (ritual). The Hebrew scholar William Robertson Smith proposed that ritual was the primary expression of religious awareness that over time came to be replaced by myth.[10] Like others of his day, most notably Sir James George Frazer the anthropologist,[11] he was heavily influenced by the evolutionary theory that assumed humans were gradually getting wiser, and the dominance of cognitive propositions provided evidence for that because words (myth) are self-evidently superior to primitive deeds (rituals). Over the ensuing decades that idea was seriously undermined by the barbarities of two world wars and no one today would believe that we are on a trajectory of continuous moral and spiritual improvement, indeed many would argue the opposite. The relationship between myth and ritual is undoubtedly more complex than that but it is beyond dispute that in the Bible, words and actions – especially actions that might in some way be regarded as 'sacramental' – go together.

An example would be in Mark 7.31–37 where Jesus' ritual actions of spitting, touching the tongue of a man with no hearing or speech, and sighing are accompanied by the word *Ephphatha*. Then there is the ministry of John the Baptist, who accompanies the ritual of baptism with a statement that articulates its significance (Mark 1.4–8), followed by a similar pattern in the Great Commission of Matthew's Gospel, where 'making disciples' and 'teaching' are natural accompaniments of the actual ritual experience (Matthew 28.18–20). Similarly, in a context that was itself intrinsically ritualized, Jesus not only shared bread and wine with his disciples but offered them an explanation of its greater significance

(Mark 14.22–25) – a combination of doing and telling that was reflected in the Passover tradition itself as ritual actions involving clothing and various artefacts for a journey were combined with questions and answers about the original story to transform what might otherwise have been a meal with dressing up into a (sacramental?) encounter with the divine. There are other passages, of course, where the combination of ritual and story is not overtly present, but which point in the same direction to suggest that this combination is in essence the thing that transforms something ordinary into something transcendent. An example would be the story of the couple on the road to Emmaus, whose lives are turned around by a ritual action on the part of Jesus, apparently without any explanation being offered (Luke 24.13–35). But in that context, the story was already known to the couple, and Jesus' action of blessing their meal brought to mind what they already knew.

Returning now to some of the questions I raised in the stories with which this chapter began, that would seem to be the clue as to how and why some of them were sacramental for those who were involved. In the training course for social workers, the sharing of bread and melted ice water/wine made a natural sacramental connection for those who were familiar with the biblical narrative, and it potentially became so for others as those who knew the story shared it with them. Otherwise it was just an interesting way to end a day of professional development. Something similar occurred with Barni's Feast where, though everything was in mime and therefore the focus was entirely on ritual action rather than the story behind it, everyone present was already well familiar with the story and made that connection quite naturally. Interestingly, some of them commented that the absence of words was what made it especially meaningful to them as it created a space in which to appreciate the essence of the Eucharist in new ways, and for them it became doubly sacramental as it were.

The other two stories offer insights from a different, more obviously missional, perspective, and for that reason pose a challenge to our understandings of the sacramental. Though the creative use of bread and water had obvious resonance with aspects of the Christian tradition, neither of them used these items in a way that might have been anticipated. The sharing of bread at *Fridays in Faith* emerged out of the sense of brokenness felt by so many people in today's world, and through the broken bread made a connection from that to the brokenness of God on the cross. And the invitation to pour water over a worshipper at Fuller Seminary so she would be soaked from head to toe similarly emerged out of her desire for a new beginning and a sense that this would somehow facilitate that. The prime catalyst here was not a connection with a pre-existent Bible narrative that would give legitimacy to what was happening and enable it to be regarded as sacramental. Rather, the catalyst here was human need, or more precisely, a consciousness that there was something that could take people beyond a sense of need and to a space where they could be transformed through an encounter with the Spirit of God. The story here was what, in other places, we might describe as the *missio Dei*: God at work in the lives of ordinary people.

While the notion of the *missio Dei* has become a catchphrase of contemporary mission theology, it is not always clear what it might look like in practice. If it is correct that the story is the thing that denotes otherwise ordinary experiences as vehicles of divine grace, then it is legitimate to ask which story we are referring to. Undoubtedly, the Bible stories will be one component, but if the *missio Dei* is – as we say – also a part of God's story (what God is doing in the world today), and if that in some way relates to the story of our lives, inviting us to fresh encounters here and now, then we need to ask how we might take that contemporary story seriously as a means of grace and, consequently, of a broader understanding of sacrament as a transformational experience of God-in-Christ. Augustine has an interesting passage in which he reflects on Jacob's wrestling with the angel and highlights the ambiguity inherent in the very word 'sacrament': 'How might we compare the power of an angel and that of a mortal? It is a mystery; therefore it is a *sacrament*; therefore it is a *prophecy*; therefore it is a *metaphor*; therefore *let us understand*.'[12] Mystery-sacrament-prophecy-metaphor offers a wide range of possible connections, and indeed Augustine himself listed more than 300 typical sacramental experiences, so we might well ask how we have ended up with such a constrained understanding of the freely given grace of God.

To address the missional challenges of our culture we need to rediscover the question that Philip asked of the Ethiopian: 'Do you understand what you are reading?' (Acts 8.30) – a question that will be a good deal more complicated for us to answer than it was for him, as today very few are reading the Bible. But they are finding the narrative of their lives in films, novels, music, sport, social media friendships, and more besides. The prevalence of big questions of meaning in many of these media is itself a sign of the spiritual search of our generation and arguably this is part of the *missio Dei*, what God is doing in the world. What would the sacramental narrative look like if we included not only what God has done in the past but also what God is doing now through these new stories? Does God always do the same thing, or is the 'new thing' so often promised in Scripture (Isaiah 43.19 etc.) still a work in progress? Can we invoke the slogan of seventeenth-century Dutch pietist Jodocus van Lodenstein, 'Reformed and Reforming' in support of such a quest? And have we too easily relegated process theology to the backwaters of missional reflection? These and similar questions might not provide any definitive answers, but they could take us in fresh and creative directions of travel as we seek to connect our own creativity with the Creator in what Michel de Certeau calls the practice of everyday life.[13]

Notes

1 Andrew M. Greeley, *God in Popular Culture*, Thomas More Press, Chicago, 1988, p. 15.

2 Augustine, *Sermons* 272.

3 For a more extensive description of this event, see John and Olive Drane, *Reformed, Reforming, Emerging and Experimenting*, Church of Scotland, Edinburgh, 2011, pp. 19–22. Available at http://www.churchofscotland.org.uk/__data/assets/pdf_file/0015/5811/ga11_emerging_reformed.pdf – accessed 29 September 2016.

4 James F. White, *The Sacraments in Protestant Practice and Faith*, Abingdon Press, Nashville, 1999, p. 13.

5 For a more extended reflection on this event, see Olive M. Fleming Drane, *Clowns, Storytellers, Disciples*, Bible Reading Fellowship, Oxford, 2002, pp. 72–4.

6 John Wesley, *The Sermons of John Wesley*, sermon 16.

7 See Ian Bradley, *Water: A Spiritual History*, Bloomsbury, London, 2012.

8 Each day a procession brought water from the Pool of Siloam into the temple where it was poured out as part of the ritual, recalling the occasion when Moses got water from the rock, which was the historical period of Israel's life that Tabernacles also celebrated. This was not the only point at which the creative arts played a significant role in the feast: Mishnah *Sukkah* IV.9 records how 'Pious men danced with torches in their hands and sang songs of joy and praise, while the Levites played all sorts of instruments. The dance drew crowds of spectators for whom grandstands had been erected. It did not end until the morning at a given sign, when water from the spring of Shiloh was poured over the altar.'

9 Joshua 4.21.

10 William Robertson Smith, *Religion of the Semites*, A & C Black, Edinburgh, 1894. The lasting significance of this work is reflected in the fact that a new edition with introduction by Robert Segal was published as recently as 2002.

11 James George Frazer, *The Golden Bough*, Macmillan, London, 1890. Published as two volumes in its original edition, but then expanded and rewritten so that by 1915 it comprised twelve volumes. And, like William Robertson Smith's work, it is still in print in various critical editions.

12 Augustine, *Sermons* 122.3.3. The choice of language was not incidental: 'mystery' was the Greek word originally used to describe what in Latin became 'sacrament', a word that in turn was closely related to 'figura' (metaphor) and 'prophetia' (prophecy). Cf. W. A. Van Roo, *The Christian Sacrament*, Gregorian and Biblical Press, Rome, 1992, pp. 38–43.

13 Michel de Certeau, *The Practice of Everyday Life*, University of California Press, Berkeley, 1984.

PART 2

Sacraments in Formation and Worship

[Being led by the Holy Spirit,] Philip began to speak, and starting with [the words of the prophet Isaiah,] he proclaimed to [the Ethiopian Eunuch] the good news about Jesus. As they were going along the road, they came to some water; and the eunuch said, 'Look, here is water! What is to prevent me from being baptized?' He commanded the chariot to stop, and both of them, Philip and the eunuch, went down into the water, and Philip baptized him. (Acts 8.34a–38)

Therefore, since we are receiving a kingdom that cannot be shaken, let us give thanks, by which we offer to God an acceptable worship with reverence and awe; for indeed our God is a consuming fire. (Hebrews 12.28–29)

Introduction

Reagan Humber's Chapter 4 reminds us that mission to the dechurched begins with assisting those who have been abused or harmed by church, to shift to reconstructing faith, where the sacraments are a medium for people to experience God's love as the beginning of a renewed discipleship. Reagan gives great insights into how sacramentality allows people to grow in the experience of receiving the love of God, and therefore grow in confidence of their renewed faith. In turn, this then is a great encouragement for the unchurched to join in this finding or restoring of faith.

Stephen Hance's Chapter 5 asserts that the traditions of sacraments and sacramental worship can be evangelistic in themselves if they are contextualized, and can play their part in embedding a fresh expression of church from fragile early stages into something more sustainable. Rightly he challenges the idea that everything needs to be new in a fresh expression; actually when used correctly and where relevant, traditional approaches to liturgical forms of sacramental worship can be very powerful.

4

Developing a Sacramentality at the House for All Saints and Sinners, Denver Colorado

REAGAN HUMBER

Our context

House for All Sinners and Saints (HFASS) is a congregation of the Evangelical Lutheran Church in America (ELCA) in Denver, Colorado. HFASS was founded in 2008 as a seminary project by the Reverend Nadia Bolz-Weber in partnership with the Rocky Mountain Synod of the ELCA. HFASS was founded by Bolz-Weber as a community where people like herself could hear the good news of Jesus without having to culturally commute. With her mixture of tattoos, foul language and former experience with drugs and alcohol (she has been in recovery for years), Bolz-Weber began HFASS as a monthly gathering in her living room for those who felt unwelcome in more mainstream church settings. Eventually, HFASS outgrew the monthly gatherings and began meeting for Eucharist every Sunday evening, sharing space in an old Lutheran church building with a Native American congregation. In 2014, HFASS officially organized as a congregation of the ELCA and began the process of hiring its first full-time pastor, since Bolz-Weber began the church in her living room. Currently in our fourth location, HFASS now meets in the parish hall of a former synagogue (today owned by a thriving Evangelical Christian congregation) with an average Sunday attendance of around 220. We are located in a downtown, inner-city neighbourhood that is on the fault line between aggressive gentrification and deeply entrenched urban poverty. Having moved to our current location only ten weeks ago, we are in the process of learning who we are and what God's mission is for us in our current context. What we have learned thus far is that God is leading us to continue gathering as a sacramental community around our shared values of Anti-Excellence and Pro-Participation in all aspects of proclaiming the gospel, while also seeking to know Jesus in our neighbours with whom we share this part of our city.

Sacramentality at HFASS

While some of our participants (or housemates)[1] come from more explicitly sacramental backgrounds (e.g. Roman Catholic, Anglican/Episcopal, High Church Lutheran), most of our participants come from evangelical and other Church backgrounds where it would be rare to hear the term 'sacrament' or 'sacramental' (except in a pejorative, anti-Roman Catholic sense). Therefore, the introduction and evolution of sacramentality at HFASS has had to develop in a careful, attentive, intentional manner. Even for our participants who grew up in a culture of sacraments, a large number were marginalized in their former faith communities and the sacraments were often used as an instrument in that marginalization. Communion has been denied, marriages forbidden, funerals refused, vocations unrecognized and the sick and dying have been neglected. Thus, the many souls who make up HFASS, come to us with a high degree of trauma and suspicion related to the official rites of the Church (however they are defined).

The birth of a sacramental practice: anointing and healing prayer

I am an Episcopal priest serving in a Lutheran congregation, and during my interview with the search committee, we discussed what the choice to have an Episcopal pastor would mean. The discussion pointed to a number of implications, but the committee spoke most enthusiastically about the development and deepening of sacramental practice at HFASS, particularly with regard to anointing. Therefore, the practice of anointing was born out of a need recognized and named by the laity, which is a cornerstone of all sacramental practice at HFASS. Though we lean into the sacramental rites that have been handed down to us by the universal Church, the way these sacraments are lived out is always in response to the congregation's need and desire for a richer sacramental life.

Moreover, the sacramental practices we make use of during public worship also take shape in the everyday life of the congregation. If we chose to incorporate a sacramental practice, like anointing, into the Sunday Eucharist, it has been our practice that we first make use of the sacramental practice in our more ordinary moments. For example, when I visit the sick and dying, I always bring holy oil and the Ministry of the Sick from the Book of Common Prayer. I then share the administration of the oil with everyone who is present. We read the official words of the rite together and then each anoints the person in turn, using their own words of administration. Therefore, by the time we arrived at the day when anointing became a part of our public worship, many of our parishioners had already seen and even participated in the practice.

Sacramental practices as a bridge between liturgical and spontaneous prayer

As discussed above, many of the HFASS parishioners, or housemates, come from conservative evangelical and other church settings where the primary spiritual practice is spontaneous prayer. Thus, it's not uncommon for a parishioner to request that I 'pray with them' during the Sunday liturgy or a private meeting. There is obviously nothing wrong with spontaneous prayer, but so many come to our liturgies because they are hungry to discover their own individual faith experience in the collective, ancient wisdom of the Church. Therefore, when I 'pray with' my parishioners, I always begin with anointing and/or laying on of hands, beginning with the prayers in the Prayer Book. Only after the common prayers have been said, do I then add my own spontaneous words and then I often ask the parishioners to add their words as well. This hybrid practice of blending the liturgical common prayer with spontaneous prayer helps bridge the evangelical–liturgical gap. Furthermore, blending the two forms of prayer creates another opportunity to knead our sacramental practices into the rhythms of daily life.

Sacramentalism growing from pain and negative experiences of the Church

Sacramental practices at HFASS have largely been shaped by the trauma of being human. It's what we call the brokenness of humanity in Christianity, or the 'Fall'. My friend Sara Miles once said to me, 'It's really hard being a soul that has a body!' All of us are struggling with our tendency to screw up and the unending walls we run up against in daily life. We're also all at the mercy of the limitations of our institutions, including the Church. Many of our participating members are emerging from Christian fundamentalism and were quite involved in their previous churches until they found themselves unwelcome for a variety of reasons, including coming out as a LGBTQ person, a divorce, beliefs about the role of women in ministry, political convictions, addiction, mental illness, disability and theological differences. Therefore, many come to HFASS with not only a bad taste in their mouth from church, but their sense of self-worth and human dignity has been deeply wounded. The sacred violence that the Church has inflicted on its own is always in the room, when we make liturgy together. However, I bristle at the idea that HFASS is a church for those who have been wounded by the Church, as if our primary purpose were to be a spiritual ER for the rest of the Church so that we can get 'them' healthy again, so that 'they' can get back to the Church again. No. At HFASS, we're much less interested in those who have been wounded by the Church and much more interested in those who have been wounded by being human. And I'll give you a hint – that's all of us! HFASS does not exist to be an apology for the Church, but rather, as a sign of the ridiculously radical way that God takes in the mess of all our lives and then makes something beautiful. And since we're all messed up, then one thing's for sure – we're all in this together. Therefore, our liturgy must reflect the we're-all-in-this-togetherness of the good news of Jesus Christ. 'There is no longer Jew or Greek, there is no longer slave or free, there is no longer male and female; for all of you are one in Christ Jesus.' In terms of liturgy, we understand Paul to also mean, 'There is no longer clergy or lay, there is no longer altar guild or newcomer, there is no longer licensed eucharistic visitor or concerned friend', for we are all doing this Body of Christ thing together.

What does this then mean? For one, it means we have no 'highly trained' groups of people who are set aside for privileged responsibilities in the liturgy. Altar guild, for instance, is whoever signs up from month to month to bake bread and set the altar. We put out a jobs board every month that lists various jobs like altar guild, greeter, set up, clean up and so on. Anyone can sign up, including a first-time visitor, which means – take a deep breath – a newcomer could visit for the first time one week and be on altar guild the next! And, yes, that has happened. It happened just last month, in fact. And you know what? It worked! Thanks be to God, we have one more person caring for God's table, who might have believed herself before to be unworthy of such a duty.

That's how this making liturgy together works. The work is no longer owned by those who have demonstrated themselves worthy of it. The work of reading Scripture, setting the table, minding the coffee, or even praying the collect of the day, all of it is owned by all who show up with arms outstretched saying, 'Here am I.'

Does this mean that sometimes the liturgy is a lot less seamless? Sure. At HFASS, most of the spoken parts of the liturgy are said by those who show up and grab the corresponding worship booklet. We have stacks of booklets at the entrance and some of them have jobs assigned to them: reading the Gospel, announcements, prayers of the people and so on. Though folks usually figure out what to do, sometimes we'll stand around awkwardly waiting for John to remember to walk up to the lectern or Rick won't realize there's a typo in the prayer we read EVERY WEEK and so he prays for 'ducks who are suffering' instead of the 'sick and suffering'. But we just laugh and those liturgies always turn out to be the best.

Open table

At the beginning of our liturgy, we always announce: 'Here at HFASS, we have an open table, which means that everyone, without exception, is invited to come forward for Communion, which for us is the Body and Blood of Christ.' By open table, we not only mean that all are welcome to receive Communion, but all are welcome to administer the sacrament as well. Communion servers may be children (usually with their parents assisting), newcomers and even the unbaptized. I had a hard time with the last example when I first came to HFASS as pastor. It ruffled my seminary-groomed feathers to serve Communion next to someone who I knew wasn't baptized. However, over time, I realized that not a single person who served Communion did so and then disappeared. Everyone who has served Communion has returned and gotten increasingly involved. Watching these newcomers stick around led me to stop listening to the critical voice and to shift my attention to the following question: Does opening the administration of a sacrament to all invite the participant into a deeper relationship with the Body of Christ? The answer has been a resounding 'Yes' in our context. That's all I needed to know.

On the Feast of the Baptism of Our Lord, I preached a sermon on the open font. In the sermon, I noted that we say we have an open table, but do we also have an open font? In light of our practice of allowing all to administer sacraments, the answer must be 'Yes'. The font is open. God's promises in the waters of baptism are always already for everyone, and thus, we cannot, in good faith, use baptism as a litmus test for participation in the Church. But does such open participation in the sacraments water down baptism (pun intended)? I'll conclude by answering this question with something that just happened in a HFASS liturgy.

Every year on Baptism of Our Lord, we make an open call to baptism. Channelling our evangelical brothers and sisters, we literally invite any who wish to come forward for baptism. There's no class. No exam. No testimony. Just the pure desire to claim God's promises as one's own. This year, two women came forward for baptism. Both were newcomers and gay. One was in her 30s and was raised Jewish. The other was in her 20s, was raised evangelical and was attending HFASS for the very first time. She's not missed a Sunday yet. These baptisms bring our number of baptisms in 2017 to five, and it's only the first week in February (at the time of this writing).

At HFASS, we don't claim to know exactly how God works, but we know that God is at work. We just try and get out of the way so that Grace can flow freely.

Formation of sacramental ministers

After months of incorporating anointing into the ordinary moments of life inside and outside liturgy, we began preparing to include anointing and healing prayer as a regular component of our public worship. Before jumping into the practice, we started with formation. Over the course of a few months, we held a few workshops on anointing. In these workshops, we discussed the history and meaning of anointing, the practical aspects of anointing (the words of administration, how to make the sign of the cross, what supplies are needed for cleaning, etc.) and we practised how anointing would take place within the Sunday liturgy. We also regularly hold workshops on listening and confidentiality. Thus, the sacramental practice of anointing developed within a larger context of lay pastoral care. At HFASS, we don't set aside a special group of people and call them our Pastoral Care Team. Instead, we see pastoral care as the responsibility of the entire community. We therefore train anyone who wishes in active listening, confidentiality, and other fundamentals of lay pastoral care.

Setting of sacramental practice

In the end, we decided to offer anointing during a time in our liturgy called Open Space. At HFASS, we follow the historic, ancient shape of the liturgy (Gathering, Confession and Absolution, Kyrie, Readings, Sermon, Prayers, Eucharist, Sending), but after the sermon, we pause for ten minutes for what we call Open Space. The assembly uses this time to sit in silence, pray at a prayer station, light a candle, write a prayer, walk around outside or to take a break for refreshments. Thus, we decided that Open Space would be the most natural place where we could incorporate anointing. Once we were ready to begin offering anointing, we added an announcement at the beginning of the liturgy to explain to the congregation what anointing is, who it's for (anyone who has a need for healing), where and when they could locate the anointing station.

Authority

Another piece of the HFASS identity is the congregation's relationship to authority, which has a direct impact on sacramental practice. Many of our housemates come to HFASS from contexts where authority has traumatized them and/or those they love. Many housemates come, often very recently, from both liturgical and evangelical churches where they have experienced excommunication and other forms of sacred violence because of their gender, sexual orientation, addiction, marital status, race or ethnicity, personal beliefs and politics and so many other parts of themselves that they seek to embody openly at HFASS. Therefore, there is always a delicate dance with authority when we seek to introduce new (or new-to-us) sacramental practices. With regard to anointing, the resistance to authority showed up around the oil itself and who the ministers of the sacrament would be. Despite being a congregation of the ELCA, the HFASS have always participated annually in the Chrism Mass at the Episcopal Cathedral in Denver, where we renew our ordination vows and obtain several bottles of blessed oil and chrism. When we first held a workshop on anointing, there was some discussion about whether we needed to use oil blessed by a bishop or even by a pastor. The participants wondered whether we could use oil blessed by a lay person. We had a robust discussion about authority in that instance, but ultimately we resolved that our unity with the universal Church is a value that is as important to the congregation, as is our value of pro-participation. Thus, we decided to continue using oil blessed by the bishop, or by the pastor if we ran out of the 'episcopal oil'. However, we also discerned that any person, lay or ordained, would administer the oil in the context of anointing in public worship. Anyone who has participated in a workshop (or has gone through an orientation to anointing) may administer the oil and lay on hands during the Sunday liturgy. When parishioners arrive on Sunday, there is now a box set out and whoever is available picks it up and waits at the anointing station during Open Space. In the box, we provide a card with the words of administration, a couple bottles of oil and the cherished package of 'holy wet wipes'. The anointing ministers preferably work in pairs and can therefore help each other if there's a crowd or if something surprising occurs. After the liturgy, the anointing ministers and a pastor debrief to talk through how it went, what they noticed and to give support for any difficulties.

Conclusion

We began offering anointing in public worship during Lent, and limited it initially to that liturgical season. During Eastertide we took a break, but quickly discovered that the congregation had come to love and expect anointing and healing prayer. Therefore, starting on Pentecost, we added anointing as a permanent, weekly sacramental practice to our Sunday Eucharist.

Every week, our anointing ministers report that there is always a line of folks hungry to hear the words that God will raise them up and make them whole. The development of anointing at HFASS is a beautiful example of how sacramental practice rises out of actual needs in the congregation and how a community with a fraught relationship to the Church can nurture traditional sacramental practices in a way that is authentic to our context. Practices that often remain the purview of the clergy or a select few do not have to stay this way. Sacramental practices can be taught and incorporated into the ordinary lives of Christians and then unleashed to be administered by all and for all. Sacraments aren't the magic spells of wizard priests, but are outward signs of inward graces that God gives to us all. The job of clergy isn't to hoard the signs of God's grace, but to share them and empower the Church to embody grace throughout our common life. Priests and pastors are needed to share the sacraments, form the laity to know the sacraments more deeply and to then give away our authority by welcoming the whole Church into the administration of our most profound spiritual practices. Our experience at HFASS demonstrates that our liturgical traditions can and should be our best tools for evangelizing a world that is hungry for the love of God made visible.

Note

1 At HFASS, we tend not to use the language of membership. When we organized as a congregation, the category of 'participating member' was added to the by-laws to encourage participation and combat the 'in vs out' dynamic of membership. A 'participating member' is defined as anyone who contributes to the work of the church through contributions of time, talent and money. All participating members are considered full members of the church and have the right to vote in congregational meetings and other official forms of congregational decision-making. All members, regardless of type, are universally referred to as housemates or participants.

5

Worship, Sacrament and Fresh Expressions of Church

STEPHEN HANCE

Early in 2015, two years into my post working as the Director of Mission and Evangelism for Southwark Diocese, I embarked on a kind of North American road trip. This was not my first road trip in the USA, but it was a trip with a different purpose from others I had taken. I had come to the USA to learn about fresh expressions of church in the sacramental tradition.

I had long been convinced about the importance of the fresh expressions movement in enabling the Church to be effective in its mission, particularly among those who were distant, not just from Christian faith, but from the whole culture and language of church life. Those of us, like me, who have grown up in church circles, have become familiar with and accepting of things which seem very odd to non-church people. Clergy in robes, community singing, recited prayers – none of these things, however good and valuable in themselves, have much resonance for most non-churchgoers. It has always seemed to me that the charge which I, like all Church of England clergy, received at my ordination, to 'proclaim the faith afresh in each generation', required some fresh and imaginative and contextual thinking in many places, to work out what church for connecting with non-church people might look like *here*. The fresh expressions movement has been about trying to take that challenge seriously.

It has also been about trying to develop communities which were both missional *and* ecclesial. In other words, the movement was not about simply trying to create stepping stones between the culture of wider society and the culture of the

Church so that non-church people could make the journey a bit more easily. To do that would be to agree that the journey towards faith was necessarily a journey into the culture of church, albeit a journey that could be broken down into small, manageable steps. The fresh expressions movement has instead insisted that the Christian faith can be planted into *any* culture, and that, when planted there, it would grow into a form of church which was *both* true to the Gospel *and* true to the culture in which it had been planted. These forms of church are not staging posts on the way to the real thing, but fully church in every respect, albeit in a way that might look very different from church as we have received it.

All of which leads directly to the question of the sacraments. If the Church is in some sense the community that is constituted around the sacraments, particularly those of baptism and Holy Communion, then those sacraments also need to be appropriately embodied and expressed in the life of every local Christian church. And yet those sacraments appeared to have a somewhat peripheral role in the life of many communities I knew which would otherwise qualify as fresh expressions, including those I had helped to begin while in parish ministry. Furthermore, I had now taken a role that gave me responsibility for encouraging the development of the fresh expressions agenda in a diocese with a fairly strong catholic tradition, where an inability on my part to help parishes reflect deeply on these matters would undermine the whole strategy. And so I headed to the USA, to find out how churches there were approaching this issue.

My trip begins in Los Angeles, accompanied by my wife Jacqui for the first few days. Our first church was Thad's, described as an emergent mission station of the Episcopal Church, in Santa Monica, led at that time by Revd Jimmy Bartz (who has since moved on). Thad's began in 2006 with about thirty people. Revd Bartz was the founding pastor. The aim of Thad's, he told me, was to create a church within the culture of a denomination – the Episcopal Church – for people who otherwise would not be attracted by denominational church.

Jimmy describes an Anglo-Catholic background which was broadened for him by his experience of seminary, placement churches, and his ordained ministry. The church had grown over the ten years of its life, although not as fast as Jimmy had expected or hoped. Attendance on the Sunday we were there was around one hundred people. Unlike the majority of the churches I visited, there was little obviously sacramental or liturgical about the worship. Jimmy told us that Holy Communion (like baptism) is celebrated 'several times a year' rather than every week. He spoke passionately about Mass as something much bigger than a service – 'it's the thing that is happening out there all the time.' One thing that was new to us, but which I had to get used to on this trip, was the dialogical sermon. Almost nowhere I visited had a traditional preach. Thad's got closest, with a 20-minute talk on a biblical text (not from the lectionary) from Jimmy, followed by open space for questions and discussion.

Later that same day we visited Mosaic in Hollywood – not strictly part of the study tour, but an interesting comparison. Mosaic is an evangelical megachurch led by pastor Erwin McManus, whose job title is 'cultural architect', aimed squarely at LA's young and beautiful people. By comparison with our morning at Thad's – and almost everything else I would visit on this trip – I was struck by how performance-y and non-participative the whole experience was, albeit of a very high quality.

Our next visit was to Holy Spirit Silver Lake. Holy Spirit meets on a Thursday evening, at the time we visited in a small arts centre, and describes itself as 'a progressive episcopal community'. Its main service is described as a 'Lord's Supper in three courses' and was, from our perspective, deeply moving. On arrival we found a room set out with candles, food, wine and beer, with an excellent jazz band playing. About twenty people, all wearing name badges, were milling about, and everyone was extremely friendly. This was the first church where more than one or two people had spoken to us. After about thirty minutes the liturgy began, a service of the Word leading into a Eucharist. We sat in a semi-circle for this, with different parts of the liturgy led by different people from their seats. The sermon was about 5 minutes of reflection followed by a somewhat overlong Open Space time for people's own thoughts and reflections. Only when someone stood to begin the Eucharist – which was celebrated on the same table from which food had been shared – was it clear who the ordained person in the room was. As was common in the churches I visited, an explicit invitation was given to all to receive the sacrament, regardless of where they might be in their own faith journey. Holy Spirit, we discovered in conversation afterwards, had grown out of a Lent Group to reach people who felt disconnected from church, particularly but not exclusively gay men. We were told that lots of clergy come to visit for their own personal refreshment, and I could understand that very well. We loved the welcome, the hospitality, and the music.

By the next Sunday we were in San Francisco, and worshipping at St Gregory of Nyssa. St Gregory's story is reasonably well-known, primarily due to the books of Sara Miles, who is on the staff team there. I had heard Sara speak at Greenbelt, which was partly why I wanted to go. St Gregory's would also definitely not call itself a fresh expression, as Sara and Rector Paul Fromberg explained to us after the service, arguing (perhaps slightly unfairly) that 'fresh expressions' tend to have a light rock twentieth-century mentality. 'We are dependent less on aesthetics and more on community.' One theme that comes out strongly at St Gregory's is mutual conversion. Sara preached on the conversion of St Paul the day we were there – it was his feast day – and argued that Ananias as much as Paul is converted: the scales only fall from Paul's eyes when Ananias is able to see him as brother. In conversation this same theme came up. St Gregory's openness to all is not, I was told, about a charism to be hospitable, but a desire to be changed, to reveal something unknown. For Paul and Sara, St Gregory's is founded on eucharistic theology. The most well-known way that is expressed is in the use of the altar not only for eating together after the service, but for their foodbank during the week. Everything, they say, relates to the altar. The open table is a theological statement, not about being inclusive but theologically sound in following Jesus who gets into trouble for sharing bread with everyone.

Our day ended at Grace Cathedral, at their Eucharist on the Labyrinth. Again, Grace is, of course, not a fresh expression. But the creative use of the labyrinth – the midweek Yoga on the Labyrinth is the Cathedral's largest gathering, with 700 people attending – was another creative example of a church being creative about using the resources of the Christian tradition to connect with the 'spiritual but not religious' who are such a large proportion of our wider community, particular among the younger urban population. From this point in the trip Jacqui had to return home and I was joined by Jonathan Clark, Bishop of Croydon.

Heading north up the west coast, we spent time in Portland and Seattle. One of the most impressive people we met on this trip was Revd Karen Ward, the founder of Church of the Apostles in Seattle and more recently of Portland Abbey. As Karen is the author of another chapter in this book, I will leave her to tell her own story. One reflection from this leg of the trip, though, was the fragility of much of what we were seeing, and a particular challenge to diocesan authorities about support and protection. We were reminded that fresh expressions may be very vulnerable particularly during their initial years, but also beyond those, if they continue to focus on engaging with those who are not familiar with church or Christian faith. Many of those people will be carrying areas of brokenness in their own lives, and most will have no understanding of Christian stewardship or the costs of running a church. Meanwhile diocesan authorities may be trying to sustain ministry on diminishing income, or have unrealistic expectations of how long it may take a new worshipping community to become self-sustaining. So pioneers may feel the pressure of the diocese expecting measurable results even as they deal with the particular stresses of their own ministry. One wonders whether greater security can be created for pioneers to allow them to get on with the work while being properly supported.

Also in Seattle we enjoyed tremendous Anglo-Catholic worship at St Paul's – not a fresh expression, but wonderful nevertheless – and I attended Vespers at George, probably the smallest and most embryonic church I visited, with a vibe almost like a home group. George sadly never quite took off, and was closed by the diocese in the summer of 2015.

I had been interested by the use of the title Vespers to describe the service at George, and surprised that there wasn't much liturgy or anything recognizably Episcopal about it. The same could not be said for Compline at St Mark's Cathedral, Seattle, the largest gathering I visited. Compline gathers 300–400 mainly younger people from across Seattle at 9 p.m. every Sunday night. Most go to no other service. Many thousands more listen online. The service is beautifully sung, and simple. The choir process out and begin to sing. Most of the congregation sit in the semi-darkness on cushions or lie on the floor around the altar. (Being a bit older than most, we took a pew!) The service is entirely non-participative until part way through when everyone stands to face the altar and recite the creed, before returning to their former position! There are no clergy visible, no preach, indeed not even a spoken welcome.

Compline is not sacramental, of course. But the service challenged almost everything I thought I knew about fresh expressions and church planting. Instead of minimizing the gap between the contemporary culture and the liturgical culture of the Church, it recognized and almost magnified it. It made no overt attempt to draw people into any further exploration of faith. As the Dean, the Very Revd Steve Thomasen, put it to me, 'It's a mission strategy that only works because it gives no hint of being a mission strategy.' Indeed the service had been started, not as a mission strategy, but because the choir wanted to sing it. That was more than fifty years ago, and a decade passed before there were more than ten in the congregation. Sometimes growth takes a long time! It also takes consistency. Compline at St Mark's Cathedral happens every week come what may. There is much to ponder in the fact that hundreds of twenty-somethings attend this most traditional of liturgical services.

From here, I flew to the East Coast and completed my tour by myself.

In Brooklyn, I visited two interesting fresh expressions, both led by very creative young women, both strongly sacramental in their own way. Bushwick Abbey, led by Kerlin Richter, was still at an early stage in its development, and has had to navigate a transition since then as Kerlin returned to Portland to take on a parish there. St Lydia's, led by Emily Scott, is becoming quite well known as 'the dinner church'. The Eucharist began with a prayer of blessing and consecration and distribution of bread with singing, then a light meal, followed by Scripture, a sermon, prayers, blessing of grape juice and distribution. After a communal clear up, there was a closing hymn, blessing and dismissal. This returns the Eucharist to its root as a shared meal, albeit in a way that many Anglicans might find difficult. Partly for that reason, Emily chose to be ordained as a Lutheran, so this is not an Episcopalian church. In common with most fresh expressions I visited, there was a strong emphasis on invitation and welcome of all, with a particular emphasis on the LGBT+ community. There was equally a focus on practice over doctrine. St Lydia's website says, 'Instead of trying to figure out what we believe, we're trying to live what we practice'. The model of discipleship therefore moves away from one in which intellectual assent comes first, to one in which the practices of the faith – among which the Eucharist is key – are seen as shaping us into disciples who are learning to believe in Christ and to live for him.

Also in New York I met Canon Stephanie Spellars, then Canon Missioner in the Diocese of Long Island and now Canon to the Presiding Bishop for Evangelism and Reconciliation. Canon Spellars first came to prominence as the founder of The Crossing, an emergent congregation at Boston Cathedral, which I was able to visit as Boston shivered under several feet of snow. I met there with the current priest, Revd Marsha Hoecker, and with the Dean of Boston, the Very Revd Jep Streit. The Crossing is now long enough established to be having to face 'second phase' questions, such as, what provision do we need to be making for children now many of our congregation are old enough to have them? What is our identity, and is it as a church in its own right or as something else? As in other places, the Eucharist was highly participative and informal, with a dialogical sermon rather than a talk, and open prayers of the people. All were invited to receive at the Eucharist, and to distribute, and in fact all stretched out their hands during the prayer of consecration. The Crossing's website talks about the Eucharist as 'the Communion meal when all the outcasts and the incasts come together'. The Crossing experienced a long transition when Stephanie moved on, and numbers dwindled as is often the case when a charismatic founding pastor leaves. To me, the community felt as if it was continuing to meet a need for a very diverse group of LGBT+, non-church, post-evangelical and many other people.

This chapter has been primarily about sharing a story. Other chapters will do more in the way of theological reflection. But a few concluding comments may be in order.

The first is simply to note the evangelistic potential of the Church's traditions for at least some of those we are seeking to engage with the gospel. It is easy to fall into the trap of thinking that fresh expressions, or missional worship more generally, must be about abandoning the traditional for the sake of the modern. The problem with this, of course, is that nothing dates more quickly than yesterday's modern. The largest congregation I saw on this visit was in the most traditional worship setting – 9 p.m. Compline in a grand cathedral hovering over Seattle.

The second is to paraphrase Leonard Cohen in his song 'Anthem' and say that sacraments are one of the ways that light gets in. They offer us a way to encounter God, not just to talk about God. Of course, that encounter can happen in all kinds of ways and all kinds of places. I take that to be what Jimmy

Bartz is talking about when he says that the Mass is taking place 'out there' all the time. And yet the dominical sacraments offer something distinct, even so – a means by which Jesus says he will be known to his people, a moment of encounter. Much of the Church's evangelism is through words, and that's good and right. But is there a place for those who are still on their journey of faith, who may not yet know exactly where that journey is taking them, to meet Jesus through the sacraments, and especially the sacrament of Holy Communion?

This is a challenge to church discipline and polity of course. Canon law in the Church of England does not permit an open table. The same is true in the Episcopal Church, as some of the clergy I met admitted to me, and yet a blind eye is often turned. When I was in parish ministry I often found myself saying, just prior to the distribution of the Eucharist, something like: 'We welcome all baptized Christians to receive.' Almost every church I visited on this visit would have said: 'We welcome all, wherever you are on your journey of faith.' In reality, of course, we give the elements to whoever presents themselves at the altar rail, often without knowing much about them. Might we want, for the sake of mission, to at least consider being more explicit about this?

Our human instinct is often to want to draw clear lines to define who is in and who is out. In set theory these are called 'bounded sets'. Potential communicants in a parish church are a bounded set – those who are baptized Christians. But set theory also talks about 'centred sets' – those defined, not by the edges, but by something at the centre and the relationship of everything else to that centre. Potential communicants, if we applied a centred-set model, could be all those who are moving towards Christ, from whatever starting point. It's a messier picture, of course. But then Cohen's song does urge us to forget our perfect offerings. Perhaps mission requires that we should live with more mess and let Jesus look after his own table. He did, after all, give bread and wine to Judas Iscariot on the night that Judas betrayed him.

I am struck, in closing, by the idea of mutual conversion, mentioned above in connection with St Gregory of Nyssa, San Francisco. The prayer of the church in mission must always be that we too should learn, that we should be converted again, that scales might fall from our eyes too.

PART 3

Sacraments in Initiation

Do you not know that all of us who have been baptized into Christ Jesus were baptized into his death? Therefore we have been buried with him by baptism into death, so that, just as Christ was raised from the dead by the glory of the Father, so we too might walk in newness of life. (Romans 6.3–4)

Now when the apostles at Jerusalem heard that Samaria had accepted the word of God, they sent Peter and John to them. The two went down and prayed for them that they might receive the Holy Spirit (for as yet the Spirit had not come upon any of them; they had only been baptized in the name of the Lord Jesus). Then Peter and John laid their hands on them, and they received the Holy Spirit. (Acts 8.14–17)

Jonathan Clark's Chapter 6 opens up the importance of sacraments as the means by which we experience God's love, and how vital it is to use sacraments to express the 'shocking love of God' not as something awkward but, in baptism, as something wonderful and God-given. Jonathan offers a lot of liturgical advice on how the sacrament of baptism can be opened up in new contexts.

Susan Blagden's and Philp Roderick's Chapter 7 tells the story about how a fresh expression approached baptism with three very different people with different spiritual needs. Again they offer helpful wisdom in how they shaped the liturgy for such an event, and the preparation needed for those who typically are non-churched.

Ian Mobsby's Chapter 8 reminds us that we need to make sure that any candidate for confirmation is old enough to make this commitment for themselves, and that we must ensure they are not wanting this because of parental pressure to be able to get certain restricted church school places. Faith needs to be real, considered and heartfelt and not ‘dumbed down’. This is a real danger in confirmation.

6

Go and Make Disciples, Baptizing . . .

JONATHAN CLARK

God's mission to the world is embodied in a sacrament – Jesus, the original, greatest sacrament, the divine presence in a human being.[1] The good news is always about the here and now, the physical and the immediate, never the theoretical. In Jesus those of his time and place met God among them, Emmanuel. That is what Jesus is called right at the beginning of Matthew's Gospel (1.23); it is also the promise he gives at the very end of the Gospel – which is no ending at all: And remember, I am with you always.' The God who came near to us in Jesus has not gone away again. The incarnation is the mission of God into the world, revealing the world as God's creation and enabling humanity to take its place again in the divine society of which the Church is the first fruits.

The Church's mission is to invite people into the incomparable privilege of sharing in the divine life – which means to become sacramental ourselves. It's worth dwelling on the words of St Irenaeus of Lyons, one of the Church's first theologians after the apostles: 'When [Christ] was incarnate and became a human being, he recapitulated in himself the long history of the human race, obtaining salvation for us, so that we might regain in Jesus Christ what we had lost in Adam, that is, being in the image and likeness of God.'[2] St Athanasius said it even more audaciously: 'He, indeed, assumed humanity that we might become God.'[3] Salvation is a change in our whole selves to regain the original gift and intention of God that we should be in that image and likeness – our whole selves, not only a 'spiritual' component: our bodies are as much a part of what is redeemed as any other part of us. Salvation is physical because salvation is incarnational.

Christians celebrate the continuing presence of God as Holy Spirit in the life of the Church and of each believer. But for many that has become a reality which is detached from any physical experience; it is purely an inner awareness of God's presence and love. For some, it is experienced physically through the supernatural gifts of the Spirit (speaking in tongues, prophecy etc.). But there is something that lies even deeper than these, the very first of the means by which the Spirit is at work in the Church and in the Christian believer. The sacraments, and baptism particularly, lie at the heart of faith, and I want to show how baptism can also be at the heart of our mission and evangelism. If the sacraments are divided from their purpose in God's mission of love to the world, they are diminished and the Church is impoverished.

Sadly, that is what has happened, if not in theory, then in practice in the life of the Church. The sacraments are experienced as 'difficult', odd things that we do as Christians but which people can only be expected to engage with after they have joined the club. Many of those Christians who are most committed to sharing the good news of Jesus Christ are personally nourished by the sacraments; others experience them as more marginal to their own spiritual life. Regardless of their personal experiences, very few see the sacraments themselves as an integral part of their sharing in the mission of God to the world. But if the sacraments are gifts of God by which we share in God's grace, they are key sites of God's presence in the world. They are places where the miracle of God's breaking into human lives is again and again repeated.

The Church has of course created this difficulty itself, by hedging the sacraments around with increasing requirements to access them. In some churches, baptism has become understood as a marker of having 'arrived' into the Christian community. It is often conflated with 'church membership' of a particular fellowship or denomination, with all the obligations and privileges that go with membership of any organization. Baptism can therefore carry a far wider range of responsibilities than the simple repentance and faith which is preached in the New Testament. In that case it is not surprising that those who wish to reach out to the margins do not see the sacraments as a central part of their mission.

In part as a reaction to this, there has begun to be a call for an 'open table' – that access to the Eucharist should not depend on baptism. The case for this understanding of the open table is made powerfully by among others Revd Donald Schell, co-founder of the parish of St Gregory of Nyssa, San Francisco.[4] He argues that in opening Communion explicitly to all who wish to receive we are reflecting the boundary-breaking and shocking hospitality that Jesus offered to those who were the outcasts and marginalized of his day. He explicitly describes this in terms of a mission 'to follow Jesus' lead in identifying ourselves wholly with the unqualified, unprepared sinners, the socially and religiously marginalized people Jesus feasted with'.[5] He is clear that this is a step beyond 'hospitality', that is, welcoming all to our table. For Schell, the table is no longer 'ours'; it belongs to all without any further requirement than that one comes and receives: 'We could imitate Christ, do and be Christ together with any who would join us, if we acknowledged our undifferentiated, unrighteous shared claim on Jesus' presence and blessing.'[6]

I am completely at one with Donald Schell in believing that the Church must reflect the shockingly generous love of God shown in Jesus Christ, and that the sacraments of the Church demonstrate that shocking love. But in his account of the mission of St Gregory of Nyssa there is little sign of the demand that accompanies that generosity. When Jesus proclaims the good news in the Gospels, the first word is 'repent'. *Metanoia* is the word translated as repentance; many Christians then unconsciously translate 'repentance' into 'remorse'. They are quite different things. Remorse may well accompany repentance as we realize how far we have gone from God's goodness and love, but repentance itself is the act of changing, of turning around. The crowds who heard the apostles' preaching on the day of Pentecost were 'cut to the heart', full of remorse, on hearing the message about Jesus and said 'What should we do?' Peter's answer: 'Repent, and be baptized'. The remorse did not constitute repentance in itself; repentance is shown in taking the first step on the road of discipleship. Schell opens himself to the question of what it means to be a distinctive disciple of Jesus Christ – as Bishop Thomas Briedenthal puts it in his exploration of this issue:

> I wonder what we think we are doing when we extend a blanket invitation to communion with no qualifier regarding a desire to draw close to Jesus, whatever the cost.[7]

God's Spirit blows where it wills. Some dramatic stories testify to the way in which receiving the bread and wine of Communion can change lives, but exceptions do not make rules. As Briedenthal puts it, 'receiving communion is the one action in [the eucharistic liturgy] that signifies our willing union with Christ, and moreover does so quite publicly. We should not expect or ask anyone who has not crossed that threshold to partake of his Body and Blood.'[8]

The open table is in danger of creating a shortcut around the necessary stumbling block, the fact that walking in the way of Christ is also to walk in the way of his cross. Becoming part of the body of Christ means also detaching oneself from those ways of living which contradict Christian discipleship. However expressed, a choice is made, to see the cross as no longer a stumbling block, but as the foundation stone of a new life.

There is another way to open the sacramental economy to mission, which respects the dynamic of repentance. The Church needs to recover a true openness in baptism: not an open table but an open font. The font traditionally is placed near the door of the church, symbolizing its function as the point of entry into the body of Christ. It is accessible, not hidden away, not fenced off. Sacramental mission begins with re-coupling the preaching of the gospel with the act of baptism – as stated by Jesus in Matthew 28.19 and Peter in Acts 2.38, and demonstrated throughout the New Testament. 'Repent and be baptized' in the New Testament church are a natural pairing. The inward and spiritual, and the outward and physical dimensions of repentance, which Western Christians so easily detach from each other, are all part of the same action. By holding baptism back, we are depriving new disciples of one of God's gifts to them at the very time when they are most in need.

Open baptism policies have been almost as controversial as the open communion table, both in relation to children's and to adult's baptism. In this chapter it is only adults that I am concerned with, though you might want to reflect on how the argument I am making might also apply to the baptism of children who are not old enough to answer for themselves.

Different attitudes to baptism depend to a large extent on whether baptism is seen primarily in terms of the initiative of God, or primarily in terms of the faithful response of the new believer. The argument has usually been constructed by an opposition between open baptism of children and 'believer's baptism' of adults, which pushes the two approaches off in different directions. Believer's baptism is seen as an act of commitment subsequent to a faith commitment (though we all know that our journey of faith is never completed); babies and young children can clearly not express a faith of their own (though they are brought in faith by parents and godparents). When we start to think about the open baptism of adults the categories change and merge. Adults answer for themselves – but the question is where they need to place themselves on the pilgrimage of faith in order to make those answers.

Some churches are already experimenting with an approach to open baptism, announcing services at which baptism will be administered and inviting any who wish to come forward to do so. In most cases of which I am aware, this has been publicly presented in an individualistic way; there is no necessary expectation of a prior relationship with the church community. The approach I am suggesting here is very different, and based on a different view of what it means to come to faith: for me, the community of faith is key. Baptism is entry into the body of Christ, not as an abstract or theoretical entity, but embodied (I would happily also say 'incarnated') in a specific community of disciples. The open baptism I am proposing is founded around belonging, and a theology of evangelism which focuses on the community of faith as much as it does the individual believer.

When the creed is recited at baptism services in the Church of England, one of the most commonly used versions ends with this statement and response:

> Minister: This is the faith of the church.
> All: **This is our faith. We believe in one God, Father, Son and Holy Spirit.**

The candidate for baptism is then asked 'Is this your faith?', to which they reply 'This is my faith'.

To become a believer is to join in with the faith that the Church shares and proclaims. To continue in faith is to continue to live that faith. But that does not necessarily entail each individual understanding (or even agreeing with) every word at every moment of their spiritual life. During my ordained ministry, I have had numerous conversations with faithful Christians about different aspects of Christian faith which they do not understand or cannot at that moment intellectually affirm. Yet they know they are Christians, and the fruit of their faith showed in their lives. My encouragement to them was that while they continued to pray, to worship, to serve, the faith of the whole Church carried them.

I do not believe in rewriting the creeds in order to accommodate contemporary theological perceptions. But nor do I believe the creeds are a theology exam which each Christian needs to pass. They are the Church's core identity, like a sun around which we all revolve. As we grow into Christ, by the Spirit our understanding of faith should be deepened, and we are drawn closer to the God whom the creeds proclaim.

If that is the case for the ordinary life of many (maybe most) Christian people, it must surely also apply to those who come to the Church seeking faith. To be faithful is to live faithfully, not to understand a certain level of doctrine. There is a call to conversion, to repentance, which is demanding and sacrificial. It is expressed not through individual intellectual assent so much as through becoming part of a community of faith and seeking to live a life which is in accordance with the teaching of Jesus.

The open font, as I am proposing it, opens the door for the sacraments to be part of this growth in faith, rather than a reward for those how have 'made it' to a certain point of understanding. It is the sacrament of belonging at least as much as it is the sacrament of believing.

For those who have been involved in evangelistic work for any length of time, I hope that the previous paragraphs have already made the link with the now well-established idea of process evangelism. Process evangelism is the term for the recognition that most people who come to Christian faith do so gradually, through a series of influences, and over a period of time which may take months or years. That much may be uncontroversial, but it leads on to other questions, as posed by John Bowen:

> One is this: when may we say that someone has 'become a Christian'? When they are baptized? When they pray 'the sinner's prayer'? When they make public profession of faith? Should we even be asking the question at all? When we thought that the move from darkness to light was like flipping a light switch, we knew which was which. If the move to darkness to light is more like a sunrise, however, we may know when it is really dark and when the sun has fully risen, but when we may say sunrise actually happens? And, of course, does it really matter as long as the sun does rise?[9]

In the same article, Bowen goes on to suggest that within the Gospels, faith is discerned in people we nowadays might think were scarcely on the way at all. Focusing on the Gospel of John, he argues that:

> people often signal their movement towards discipleship by asking a question. More, these are normally questions which express uncertainty, doubt, and tentativeness. In John's book, such questions mean that people should be considered disciples and not just 'seekers' on the way to discipleship.[10]

He brings up five examples; to mention only one, he quotes John 7.31: 'Yet many in the crowd believed in him and were saying, "When the Messiah comes, will he do more signs than this man has done?"' The 'many in the crowd' express what John calls their belief through a question, not what we would normally think of as a statement of faith.

This article connects for me with another common theme in evangelistic thought, that belonging comes before believing. It has been widely argued that exploring faith, especially within contemporary Western society, happens most effectively within an existing community of faith. To keep people on the outside until they have made some sort of faith commitment is depriving them of the context in which such a commitment can be made. Such an approach has been criticized for reducing or even discarding the call to repentance which is integral to being a member of the Church. If the belonging that comes before believing is of the sort that makes no demand, then the criticism is justified. But as John Bowen's article suggests, the dividing line between unbelief and belief is not a clear one. In order to belong to the Christian community, what is needed is not so much a statement of individual faith as a commitment to the beliefs, values and practices of a particular community. If the church community is living out its own calling, such a commitment in itself embodies the act of repentance, because it entails living a life of worship and service. Belonging then becomes an affirmation of the Church's faith, and the demands that it makes. Baptism is how that sort of belonging is expressed.

The Church of England recently approved alternative questions to be asked of candidates (or their sponsors) at baptism services. These are:

> Do you turn to Christ?
> **I turn to Christ.**
> Do you repent of your sins?
> **I repent of my sins.**
> Do you renounce evil?
> **I renounce evil.**

There was considerable controversy over these promises, precisely on the grounds that they reduced to (or for some, beyond) a bare minimum the doctrinal commitment that candidates were expected to make. Thinking of these promises in the context I am suggesting may open up another way of understanding them, and of where we might place baptism in the journey of faith.

If baptism is the act by which people are welcomed as fellow pilgrims on the journey, these questions should mark the lowest possible threshold which is compatible with wanting to belong to the community of Jesus – turning away from evil and following in the path of Christ. This is not an accommodation to pastoral necessity or a giving up on the richness of the faith. Baptism begins a process which is life-long: Gregory the Great's famous words about the Bible give us the picture: 'Scripture is like a river again, broad and deep, shallow enough here for the lamb to go wading, but deep enough there for the elephant to swim.'[11] Baptism is the opening of the door to faith. Those baptized need only to show and say they are committed to this path and no other.

How might all this work out in practice? One way in which I could envisage it happening would be for the possibility of baptism to be an integral part of normal Christian worship. Traditional eucharistic services usually begin with a penitential rite; as the congregation meet they confess their sins and receive the assurance of God's forgiveness. In the Roman Catholic liturgy, the asperges (sprinkling with holy water) can take the place of the penitential rite.

Building on these existing elements of the Church's liturgy, we might perhaps find ourselves doing something like this:

> The congregation gathers around the font, sharing with one another what has been good and bad since they have last met; they begin to reflect on how they are as individuals and a community in their pilgrimage of faith.
>
> The service begins with an acknowledgement of God's presence, and a greeting of one another.
>
> The community reflect together on their calling as God's baptized people, reminding themselves of why they have come together.

Any who wish to be baptized will already be known and recognized as seekers within the church community. At any service (though preferably before it begins!) they may signify that they wish to join the community as it states again its baptismal identity and receive baptism themselves.

As part of its rite of repentance (rather than penitence), the community as a whole restates its faith, sharing in a creedal statement and answering together questions such as those listed above. All are then signed, or sprinkled with the same water which is used to baptize.

Any who are already baptized, and wish to be newly seen as members of the community, could join with the whole community in this renewal. Recognizing the significance of that act within the liturgy might help to meet the pastoral need of those who would otherwise feel a desire to repeat their baptism, recognizing that consciously or not they have already received the gift.

The service then continues, the newly baptized fully part of the church community.

In traditional Anglican practice, the sacrament of initiation is completed at a later date by confirmation at the hands of the bishop. Within the framework of sacramental mission that I am suggesting, that division might find a renewed purpose and power, but only if it were accepted that confirmation was not required before the baptized could receive Communion. The Church of England already recognizes that baptism is sufficient initiation to join in the Eucharist through the increasing acceptance of Communion before confirmation for children. In the pattern I am proposing, confirmation could take its place as the opportunity for those who are baptized to articulate more fully their understanding of the faith, and to commit themselves to full and active participation in the life and mission of the Church. Confirmation would mark another significant milestone on the continuing pilgrimage of faith which all God's people are part of, a pilgrimage in which 'initiation' is not a moment but a process.

Why do all of this? As I stated at the beginning of this essay, the primary reason is that God is at work through the Holy Spirit in the sacramental actions that we perform as a Church. But there are more contextual reasons too. It may also be that in contemporary Western society, sacramental mission can speak to our society in a way that more word-based approaches cannot. Symbolic action can offer a physical and emotional, as well as a rational response to the sense of disconnection from one another and the world which is one of our age's deepest spiritual needs. This is mission which begins with the Church and with community, rather than with the individual. It brings us into relationship with God through meeting with the people of God, and meeting the God who gives himself in the ordinary things of this world, water, bread and wine. It is good news for the whole human condition, the whole person we are called to be in Christ.

Notes

1 I'm following many theologians here. The most famous is Edward Schillebeeckx, who wrote 'The man Jesus, as the personal visible realization of the divine grace of redemption, is the sacrament, the primordial sacrament, because this man, the Son of God himself, is intended by the Father to be in his humanity the only way to the actuality of redemption.' *Christ, the Sacrament of the Encounter with God* (1963), p. 15.

2 Irenaeus, Against Heresies, 5. 1. 1.

3 Athanasius, On The Incarnation, 54. 3

4 Donald Schell, 'Discerning Open Table in Community and Mission', in *Anglican Theological Review* 94:2, pp. 245–55. Accessed online at www.anglicantheologicalreview.org/static/pdf/articles/schell_.pdf, 16.8.16.

5 Schell, 'Discerning Open Table', p. 252.

6 Schell, 'Discerning Open Table', pp. 252–3.

7 Thomas E. Breidenthal, 'Following Jesus Outside: Reflections on the Open Table', *Anglican Theological Review* 94:2, pp. 257–62, 260. Accessed online at www.anglicantheologicalreview.org/static/pdf/articles/breidenthal__.pdf, 16.8.16.

8 Breidenthal, 'Following Jesus Outside', p. 262.

9 John Bowen, 'Process Evangelism and The Significance of Questions in The Gospel of John', http://institute.wycliffecollege.ca/2002/04/process-evangelism-and-the-significance-of-questions-in-the-gospel-of-john/. Accessed 17.08.16.

10 Bowen, 'Process Evangelism'.

11 *Moralia* to Leander [4], 178.

7

In at the Deep End: Transforming Initiation

SUSAN BLAGDEN AND
PHILIP RODERICK

From the beginning of the *Way of Christ-likeness*,[1] it began to take root in the hearts, minds and mission of the first followers of Jesus. From then until now, there has been a quest to understand as well as to follow, to discern as well as to disciple. What is the meaning of these extraordinary teachings and events? What were the breakthroughs that shaped a testament that is clearly new?

The apostles and first disciples knew that they were not only receivers of the Word and the Way. They were also called to embody and present the Wisdom as it is in Jesus. And not only in Jesus Christ, but in the community within God we call Trinity. This is the three-in-one emergent truth as it is in the Father, the Source of all being; in the Son, the incarnate, crucified and risen Christ; in the power, gentleness and comfort of the Holy Spirit.

The flow and form of the journey of faith evolved in the months, years, decades and centuries of Christian belief and practice. It served to encourage and challenge, inspire and shape generations of followers of Jesus. Perhaps inevitably, over the course of time, interpretations and understandings of what it means to be 'in Christ' would begin to differ, sometimes markedly.

Interestingly, in the case of baptism, there has been in general, a marked convergence of focus and explanation. Baptism is the point of initiation into the community of believers gathered and dispersed in the name of Jesus. This sacrament is a primary launch-pad for all followers of Christ in faith and freedom. So it proved to be in Contemplative Fire's transformative journey of small group resourcing for baptism. We shared together in an 18-month preparation period culminating in the baptism of Linden, Luke and Simone as an integral part of Contemplative Fire's Easter liturgy.

Many years ago, in conversation with Metropolitan Kallistos Ware, one of the leading theological and spiritual voices in the Eastern Orthodox Church, Bishop Kallistos said forcefully: 'Tradition needs always to be dynamic. Once it ceases to be dynamic, it becomes traditionalism.' This key insight needs to have critical and sustained reference across the denominations of inherited church and in the emergent Christian communities. There is an ever-present need to promote and validate a healthy regard for creative imagination and the interplay of structure and spontaneity. This vibrant dimension of faith has remained figural for Contemplative Fire. In the context of our participation in the lineage of Christian discipleship, our commitment as Contemplative Fire has been to value and validate this transformational approach to Scripture and tradition, to spirituality and outreach, to wonder and worship.

> A holy man of God brings his whole self as well as the entire world to God . . . The entire work of the Church is the collaboration of the divine and the human.[2]

This far-reaching and yet eminently practical wisdom, within the great spiritual tradition of the one Church, East and West, has been formative at many levels. It undergirded our design and facilitation of the preparation process and the celebration of the baptismal liturgy within the Contemplative Fire community.

The three explorers seeking baptism came from markedly different backgrounds. One was an atheist with a very dualistic approach to life, and was particularly challenged about the darkness evident in the world. One came from a Buddhist background, who had 'accidentally' stumbled into one of our Contemplative Fire (eucharistic) Gatherings where there was a personal encounter with the risen Christ which then led to a seeking of baptism. The third one had an extraordinary, and totally unlooked for, encounter with Jesus on Glastonbury Tor. This lead to an exploration of Christian faith within the Contemplative Fire community. None of these had received any formal teaching earlier in their lives about Christian faith so the preparation for baptism needed to include some engagement with Scripture, key Christian beliefs as well as Anglican practices.

Contemplative Fire seeks to be a Community of Christ at the Edge. It was therefore only right and proper that the preparation for a reimagined baptismal service also included conversations with: the relevant bishops who had oversight and interest in what we were doing; the Development Group of Contemplative Fire; and a wider group of Companions (members), most of whom had already been baptized in other church contexts. Some interesting and differing perspectives emerged that we will explore in the remainder of the chapter. These differences proved the value of taking time to have wider conversations. The wisdom in engaging with all the stakeholders helped to shape the process as well as the final liturgy. The preparatory work produced a six-week online Lent course which helped all Companions of Contemplative Fire to engage with the baptismal liturgy and tradition.

However, as we embarked on this formational process, there was no clear plan or timetable. We met monthly for an evening and thought we might do this for nine months. In the event, it was eighteen!

An extract from one of our emails to the baptismal explorers/candidates serves to highlight the approach:

> We ask you to do some homework in preparation for the session. We invite you to help us in our shaping of the liturgy to hopefully create something that is of resonance for you while also honouring the pattern of the Church of England's baptismal liturgy. You will find below the Baptismal questions as currently included in the baptismal liturgy. We would be glad if you would read them and, in true Contemplative Fire

> fashion, wrestle with the language and theology that is really meant to be underpinning this celebration of faith. It would be great if you could then be attentive to what might emerge for you as genuine questions and answers. These would be honest markers of intent for you as you seek baptism. Please write these out and then bring them to the next session willing to share them. This will be a tremendous help, and hopefully, an inspiration too.

Indeed, each explorer shared some very personal stories reflecting their particular journeys. Each made astute and rich contributions to the discussions and discernment of the language and symbolism to be used in the liturgy on Easter Day.

Diving in: the journey and how to shape the liturgy

Contemplative Fire values listening in an attentive way to each other. On the first session each candidate was asked to tell their story of what had brought them to seek baptism. We were mindful from Scripture that those who came to John the Baptist for those first baptisms came from a very diverse range of backgrounds with different stories to tell. Christ's own journey was different again. Key reasons that emerged for these candidates were: 'I felt drawn to the Person of Christ, with no way of knowing how I could approach him, although I sensed that the way would be an inward one'; 'Where do I abide in You and You in me?' and 'I realized in that moment, in trying to find the answers I so desperately sought through my previous spiritual journeys, that I had turned further away from the one thing I truly sought, which was to know love; there was in that moment nothing to do and nowhere to go.'

The language of our liturgy was fashioned from a deep personal and group wrestling with the Jesus journey. This involved us all in a re-imagining of the ancient language and baptismal significance of the Word, the Way and the Wisdom of God. This life-enhancing task found expression in the three renunciations and in the phraseology of the baptismal questions and responses. In this context, each of the candidates prepared their stories of their journeys into faith. They initially shared these with the baptism preparation group and then later with all those gathered for the Easter Liturgy. One story was named 'From self-reliance to relationship'. Another was entitled 'From self-isolation to belonging'. The third offering was 'From self-disintegration to wholeness'. Robust, rich and real personal narratives.

The three renunciations that we arrived at and which were shared and articulated both by the explorers and by the whole congregation were as follows:

> **Renunciation 1:** Do you resist the allure of self-reliance and choose to trust in God?
> Candidates: I resist the allure and choose to trust in God.
> Gathered people: I resist the allure and choose to trust in God.
> **Renunciation 2:** Do you renounce the deceiver and choose the way of truth?
> Candidates: I renounce the deceiver and choose the way of truth.
> Gathered people: I renounce the deceiver and choose the way of truth.
> **Renunciation 3:** Do you repent of self-imposed isolation and choose community in Christ?
> Candidates: I repent of self-imposed isolation and choose community in Christ.
> Gathered people: I repent of self-imposed isolation and choose community in Christ.

What came to be the agreed wording of the baptismal questions and responses was wrestled with by the explorers and ourselves. In a culture that promotes self and personal fulfilment almost to the exclusion of everything else, this was seen as a radical, counter-cultural stance. Insights and quotes, biblical and patristic, from the early centuries of the undivided Church, became part of our discernment of an ancient yet contemporary language of faith.

Diving in: how to engage with the Christian contemplative tradition

The turning point

For each explorer there had been powerful, clearly identifiable moments of turning to Christ. In our preparation we asked them to find space in the room and to stand in it, noticing what caught their attention and how it might connect with the stories they had just shared. Silent time for reflection was then followed by the invitation to turn 180 degrees and notice again what caught their attention, and how did that speak to them about turning to Christ? It is easy to say the words: 'I turn to Christ.' Providing time to experience this kinaesthetically honoured not only the past decision to turn but also added fresh impetus to go on turning to Christ in the realities of daily life.

One of the explorers commented: 'Am I turning, or choosing to turn, or being turned by the hand of God?' Another explorer remarked: 'A sunflower turning towards the sun needs the sun to shine.' One of the explorers said: 'I'm interested in how I can die into Christ . . . The Holy Spirit is subtle, helping me find a sense of myself, my true self; who I really am. The water washing over me is taking me out of the limitations of my selfhood.'

The Renunciations in the liturgy were all said while facing west. The gathered people then all turned to face east. We were reminded of John 20 where Mary Magdalene turns in the garden to face the risen Christ and hears Christ call her by name, awakening her to who she was most truly called to be.

In the Decision, this led to a commitment not only to turn to Christ but actively to seek to live out this uniting of self to Christ, moment by moment. This was expressed in a simple gesture of moving the hands from the crown of the head, over the forehead, until they rested over the heart centre. The bodily engagement was a powerful reminder that Christianity is an incarnational faith.

The wording for each of the questions and responses that emerged for our Easter Liturgy and Baptism led directly to the generous pouring of the water over the baptismal candidates in turn:

Priest: (*Name*), do you believe in God, the Father and the Source, the Almighty and vulnerable One?

Candidates: **I believe.**

Priest: (*Name*), I baptize you in the name of the Father.

Do you believe in Jesus Christ who was broken on the cross and transformed in resurrection?

Candidates: **I believe.**

Priest: I baptize you, (*Name*), in the name of Jesus Christ.

You have been immersed in the water and thereby buried with Christ, do you believe in the Holy Spirit breathing wisdom and life?

Candidates: **I believe.**

Priest: (*Name*), I baptize you in the name of the Holy Spirit.

This concluded with a prayer for the whole community:

You mark us with your water,
You scar us with your name,
You brand us with your vision,
and we ponder our baptism, your water,
your name,
your vision.

. . .

Re-brand us,
transform our minds,
renew our imagination,
that we may be more fully who we are marked
and hoped to be,
we pray with candour and courage. Amen.

(Walter Brueggemann)[3]

Diving in: seeking transformation

In the preparation and exploration of this prayer there was a dawning realization of the radical nature of baptism, and how the whole of life was a journey to deep wholeness. Perhaps inevitably, perhaps surprisingly, this flagged up various issues for each candidate that had happened in life that now needed to be named as places of wounding, darkness or death, and in need of the Holy Spirit's transformation and healing. For one explorer this was about living from a greater life-giving belief system rather than anticipating everything being evil. For another, it was an awareness that while there might be surface similarity between Buddhism and the Christian invitation to die to self, the Buddhist approach for this explorer still had the focus on self doing the dying! The revelation that the invitation was really about surrendering the false ego to Christ's love was deeply attractive. It was that love that another explorer knew was calling her to a strong sense of belonging which was a very new experience for her.

These stories show that each candidate took very seriously the ancient symbolism of baptism.

> Baptism is total immersion in the water of death, from which we emerge in the joy of breathing once again, of 'breathing the Spirit', for the water, changed form lethal to life-giving, embodies the resurrection power of the Spirit of which it is a natural symbol . . . The water closes over the baptismal candidate like a tomb. For the tomb to become a womb the Holy Spirit must supernaturally intervene. The Spirit given brings the human being to a new birth, clothing but with incipient and real light the whole being, the heart, the desires, all the faculties, the very senses . . .[4]

In the preparation, we had separate sessions with each explorer preparing them and leading them through a service of penitence and reconciliation. This provided space for them to know and experience something of the deep, inner transformative work of the Holy Spirit.

This then leads very naturally to a rich celebration of the anointing in baptism. Those negatives that had previously been identified were willingly buried in baptism and the explorers emerged from those waters ready to be anointed.

> Christ was anointed with the oil of gladness, that is with the Holy Spirit. The Spirit is so called because he is the source of joy. You now receive the sacramental anointing. In this way you become companions and partakers of Christ.[5]

In the extensive preparation for baptism with these explorers, we were intrigued that:

> there is an ancient tradition in the church that at the baptism of Jesus as he entered the waters, the Jordan suddenly burst into flames. So was seen the coming together of the opposites, which against their natures did not cancel each other out, but by the creator/redeemer's presence co-existed in a harmony that gave birth to new life in fire and water, Babylon and Jerusalem, Gentile and Jew, slave and free, Male and Female, good and evil. Here in community we indeed owe our existence to the One who is able to hold all opposites in tension so that all life can come.[6]

This quote had particular resonance for us as the Community of Contemplative Fire. The three explorers had been baptized into Christ and as such they knew they had a place of deep belonging. Here, differences could be held in a tension, which had the potential to give birth to new life, and to go on giving birth to new life.

In summary, the invitation to Contemplative Fire to dive in at the deep end to reimagine what a fresh expression of baptism might look like within the Church of England, was to embark on a journey of transformation. This was about the whole community being involved in different ways in doing theology together. We examined Scripture, we engaged with the dynamism of the tradition, we wrestled with theological concepts, and we honoured the shared experiences of all involved. This led to the creation of a liturgy which was rich in symbol and meaning, weaving together the ancient texts and traditions, and to help make sense of the lived experience. In the end, the

Orthodox belief expressed by one hermit summed it all up: 'We are one in Christ through our baptism. We spend the rest of our lives trying to live it out.'

Notes

A wonderful source book, not only for the baptismal process but also for the unfolding life of Contemplative Fire as a fresh expression of church, is Olivier Clement's *The Roots of Christian Mysticism* (New City, New York, 2013). From this rich treasury of Christ-centred perspective and guidance we used quotes both in the course and in the service, from the Cappadocian Fathers, from Cyril of Jerusalem's 'Mystagogical Catecheses' and from the 'Apostolic Constitutions'. In more contemporary mode we drew from the writings of Walter Brueggemann, e.g. *Awed to Heaven, Rooted in Earth.*

1 Michael Perham, *The Way of Christ-likeness: Being Transformed by the Liturgies of Lent, Holy Week and Easter*, Canterbury Press, Norwich, 2016.

2 Metropolitan of Nafpaktos, *A Night in the Desert of the Holy Mountain: Discussion with a Hermit on the Jesus Prayer*, trans. Effie Mavromichali, Birth of the Theotokos Monastery, Boeotia, Greece, 1991, pp. 25, 43.

3 Walter Brueggemann, *Awed to Heaven, Rooted in Earth: Prayers of Walter Brueggemann*, Augsburg Fortress Press, Minneapolis, 2003, p. 88.

4 Olivier Clement, *The Roots of Christian Mysticism*, New City, New York, 2013, pp. 103–5.

5 Cyril of Jerusalem, Mystagogical Catecheses, III, 2, quoted in Clement, *Roots of Christian Mysticism*, p. 106.

6 Paul R. Dekar, *Community of the Transfiguration*, Cascade Books, Eugene, 2008, pp. 68–9.

8

The Place of Confirmation in a Missional and Mixed Economy Parish

IAN MOBSBY

It has been said that confirmation is a sacrament in search of a theology.[1]

I say confirmation is a sacrament we cannot afford to miss if we are serious about authentic mission and discipleship.

The North Peckham Estate in South East London has always been a place of challenge and exclusion. The death of many, including Damilola Taylor, and those who have suffered from the effects of gangs, unemployment, racism, sexism, low wages and poverty have left their mark. This has included the recent damage to windows in St Luke's Parish Church situated in the middle of the estate, where someone had been practising shooting with their air rifle and setting the church doors on fire.

However, on this particular Sunday, there was a sense of hope. On a cold crisp sunny morning in February 2016, 22 adults, teenagers and children gathered in the church in preparation for being confirmed. All had attended an eight-week course on Christianity designed for people who had little or no understanding of the faith, but who passionately wanted to be able to be confirmed because they felt a deep commitment to wanting to follow Jesus. In all the pressure and complexity of modern life and the scarcity of money, work and educational achievement, there was something amazingly beautiful happening. A mixture of all sorts of people wanted to respond to the God of love and mission, who was and is restoring all things back into right relationship with God the Holy Trinity.

Nearly all had been baptized as children, so this was an important opportunity for many to affirm the Christian faith for themselves, to take this step of their own free will, to be seen in public as committing to being a follower of the way of Jesus.

Most were second- and third-generation settlers from West Africa and the West Indies, some were from South America and only one WASP.[2] Yet even here, with people who had to struggle to access the opportunities of modern London that most take for granted, there was something awe inspiring, hopeful and moving. There was a palpable acceptance that Jesus truly was the light in the darkness, naming a hope for the now but not fully yet kingdom of God even here in North Peckham.

So we gathered, some from the youth club that we are slowly turning into a youth fresh expression of church (with its own mission, worship, and community life) to reach out to the many young people living on the local estate. Some came from the New Monastic Community which we began in November 2015 as a fresh expression of church to reach out to the 'spiritual not religious' seekers, and arts-focused 'hipsters'. But most came from those who had faithfully attended the Sunday Morning Parish Eucharist and their extended families. Slowly this Parish Eucharist attractional church congregation was growing in its mission and hospitality to local children and families, and to the many isolated older people living in various levels of poverty.

Dutifully the then Bishop of Woolwich, Michael Ipgrave, arrived to meet with all the candidates, also noting the sense of excitement in the air. He reminded them of the importance of their decision to affirm faith but also to realize that when he was anointing them with oil, they would be receiving a blessing through the presence of the Holy Spirit. Those gathered understood that confirmation and sacramental anointing was and is an ancient practice, an invocation to the Holy Spirit, to come upon those who had committed to follow the way of Jesus to receive the love of God.

So as Christians have done for thousands of years, candidates made their confessions and commitments and went forward to receive a blessing and anointing, and something profound was happening. The annoying fact about the sacraments is that there is always something profoundly emotional and other about them in that they are somewhat frustratingly indescribable. Their nature being trans-rational in mysterious otherness makes them God's rather than ours. We do not control them, God does. Often we have no idea at all what God is doing via the Holy Spirit, which makes sacraments very exciting if we sincerely believe that mission and evangelism are about catching up with what God is doing. Bishop Michael took it very seriously that there was something deeply charismatic about this moment when as a servant, disciple and bishop he is only the vessel through which God is made present to each individual through the blessing and anointing of the Holy Spirit. Everyone I spoke to felt it but struggled to form words that named what had happened. It was the same feeling I sensed at my own adult baptism, confirmation and ordination – something significant had happened, something I sensed but could not describe or even make sense of other than I felt differently with a profound sense of love and the closeness of God.

So, I hear you ask, why is confirmation important for discipleship and mission? Why is confirmation important for fresh expressions of church?

I have to confess that until relatively recently I was cynical about the place of the sacrament of confirmation, as I couldn't find a distinct theology or imperative for it that felt authentic. I was also aware of the pressure on some children to get confirmed by their parents so that they could then access good schools and colleges run by various church organizations. This is a real issue in North Peckham, where rightly parents want to help their children to get a decent education and break out of poverty and limited opportunities. There is a real tension here with the giving of privilege, courtesy of our market society, where children have to compete to get rationed educational places. The collusion of the Church having power over people in this situation has troubled me for a long time. We should never say to families, 'I will sign your form for your child to access a school place if you start to attend church reliably every week.' This is not a strategy for mission – rather this is a form of control and I do not think it helps us evangelize and enable people to experience God of their own free will. Further, children are being put under enormous pressure by this education system to get confirmed at the age of nine and under to get ready for limited school places. I as a new parish priest came under this same pressure to take very young children who were not ready to make such an important profession of faith and clearly not out of their own desire or free will. On reflection I now strongly believe we must resist this, otherwise, confirmation becomes meaningless, which is why I think so many are questioning the authenticity of the place of a sacrament of confirmation today.

However, since I became the part-time priest of a parish needing to focus on becoming missional and planting several fresh expressions of church, I have completely changed my mind out of this experience. I now think that confirmation as a sacrament and spiritual staging post becomes a blessing and tool as we seek to foster much deeper and resilient Christian disciples to survive the complexity of our contemporary global market society.

Like so many other words, confirmation is a theological word that you will not find in the Bible. The word derives from the Latin word *confirmare* meaning to strengthen. In the early Church the three sacraments of baptism, confirmation and Eucharist were celebrated in the same service of initiation by adults coming to faith (called catechumens) at the Easter Vigil, (the Saturday Evening before Easter Sunday). The early Church took discipleship so seriously that those wanting to become 'Christian' had to attend an initiation process that included learning mission and service, particularly to the poor and hungry. This catechumenate programme of Christian formation, focused on learning, praying and doing, sometimes lasted for two or three years. So at the Easter Vigil, the catechumens descended into a pool of water where they were baptized in the name of the Holy Trinity. They then ascended, were clothed in white, and then the bishop laid hands on them and anointed them with oil. The bishop would invoke the blessing of God, that the person is 'sealed' by the Holy Spirit. They then joined the rest of the Christian community, where they participated in the Eucharist for the first time. Initiation then consisted of one event with several moments the climax being the celebration of the Eucharist.

The separation of the bishop's anointing (confirmation) from baptism occurred soon after the Christian faith became part of the Roman Empire in the fourth century. At this time Christianity spread quickly through the cities and countryside, making it impossible for the bishops to preside at every baptism.[3] The bishops in the Eastern Roman Provinces (now largely the Orthodox Churches) solved this problem by delegating all three sacraments of baptism, confirmation and Eucharist to the presbyters or priests, reserving for themselves only the blessing of the oils to be used in the religious services. The bishops of the West also delegated baptism to priests but retained confirmation as a responsibility of the bishop, particularly the anointing and laying on of hands. So bishops when travelling around fulfilled their civil responsibilities and conducted services of confirmation. Therefore in the West, the sacrament of confirmation was conducted at a later time than the sacrament of baptism, at a time when it was known that the bishop was coming to a local town to fulfil spiritual and civic responsibilities.

We remember in the ancient world that there was a great concern around the issue of human mortality and salvation, particularly of infants and younger people, so that the early Christian Church practised infant as well as adult baptism. Knowing that this book is ecumenical, I am going to skip neatly over the arguments pro and against infant baptism, other than to say if you believe that infant baptism is about acknowledging the blessing and naming of a child's life by God, then there needs to be an important stage and sacrament where a person in their own free will and knowledge, can make a decision to follow Christ. In this way, the sacrament of confirmation has two functions. First the strengthening and reaffirmation of baptism and other vows and commitments, (making it a believer's sacrament). Then second the receiving, of blessing and connection with the gift of the third person of the Holy Trinity, the Holy Spirit. So as a sacrament, the act of confirmation includes a confession of sins or selfish choices, the commitment to follow Christ, the anointing of oil and the prayers for the invocation of the Holy Spirit as a blessing on the person.

Thinking about confirmation in this way means that it comes very close to the expectation of the Bible regarding discipleship and faith. In Ephesians 2.8–9 we understand that a person becomes a Christian by God's grace through believing in Jesus by faith. Such a decision should not be taken lightly, with the realization that the expectation is for the Christian to seek to follow God every day of their life. In 1 Corinthians 2.13–14 we understand that when we accept Christ as our Lord and Saviour, the Holy Spirit takes up residence in our hearts and gives us the assurance that God is present to us and that we belong to God. Confirmation then is linked to our salvation (1 Corinthians 1.7–8), that as we seek to persevere for the whole of life in faith, eagerly awaiting for the revelation of our Lord Jesus, then God will *confirm* us as disciples to the end as a form of covenant commitment.

Theological writers in the nineteenth and twentieth centuries largely coming from the more Anglo-Catholic traditions emphasized the importance of confirmation primarily as a sacrament of the Holy Spirit.[4] In this view, the communication of the gifts of the Spirit and the location of the Holy Spirits activity are expressed in the sacraments. There has been an ongoing debate for well over 200 years between the various church traditions, with those of a more sacramental theology arguing that the sacrament of baptism without confirmation was not complete. Further, some continue to argue that in our increasingly Apostolic Age,[5] the role of the sacraments is crucial to mission, because they are about enabling people to experience the reality and blessing of God the Holy Spirit.

So how does confirmation help us missionally? Well, first I think, like baptism, confirmation contributes to a greater understanding of the journey of discipleship core to the

Christian faith. As such it is incredibly important for those who have no experience of church to understand that becoming Christian, and growing as a Christian disciple requires commitment and a process of going deeper with the faith not dissimilar to the early catechumens. Too much evangelism today has the potential to dumb-down on the faith where individuals make a few commitments on 'becoming Christian' and are then expected to coast for the rest of their lives with little input other than 'churchgoing' with little depth and challenge needed for people to become mature and fully rounded Christians. I am convinced that the problem of so many de-churched people today is because of this oversimplification that says nothing of the cost of authentic Christian discipleship. Confirmation then speaks of covenant commitments, that following Jesus is deeply fulfilling but also really hard, and that we need God's help and blessing to keep us on track. Further, confirmation offers an opportunity for those who may have turned away from their faith after receiving it as a child, to then make an outward sign or commitment to reaffirm renewed faith later in life. Confirmation then becomes a key stage for the 'un- and de-churched', the focus for fresh expressions of church regarding mission and evangelism.

Confirmation classes then have the potential to be spaces and places where individuals can dig deeper with faith. In the confirmation classes I ran, I was shocked by the lack of understanding there was of the Christian faith. So we set up 'age appropriate' small groups of adults, youth and children to help people really grapple with the critical questions and understandings of faith. This was not at all easy, partly because some held on to extremely simplistic understandings, but after much struggle, I think we did get somewhere. There is always so much more you could do. One resource that proved helpful was the course *This is our Faith* by Jeffrey John,[6] which proved a reliable resource in pictures and plain language and explanation, as something that people could take away and learn for themselves in an accessible form. For some, the eight-week course that we ran with adapted notes and discussion was too much like school, which many had experienced quite negatively as a place of disempowerment and underachievement. So in response, we tried to mix up discussion with life experience to open up fact learning with note sheets to help candidates to explore Christian formation through their own thoughts and experiences. So how we do these confirmation classes really matters. On reflection, I would like next time to use the observations of Godly Play – learning through storytelling, imagination and metaphor. The truth is there is no easy way to do this, but it must be contextual. I wish there was a simple solution to Christian formation, but I have not yet discovered it. The importance here is that we try and we learn from our mistakes. Regarding leading these teaching sessions on the necessary formation for the sacrament of confirmation, I remain a novice, with much still to learn, when I was so aware that those gathered had very little concentration skills, and could not sit still for long before getting obviously bored.

However, I am convinced that some of the areas of teaching got through: that following Jesus is not easy, that God as Trinity loves us, that faith and prayer and encounter of God are important, and that discipleship is a mixture of individual life and joining in with other Christians as a pattern of worship, mission and community. As an Anglican Christian, I hope that we struck the right balance that confirmation is both a blessing from God through the Holy Spirit as a sacrament and the call to choose faith to follow Jesus Christ as a key stage of 'becoming' Christian in a whole-of-life process.

So what did we cover in the eight weeks? Well here are the areas:

Week 1	Understanding the Hebrew Scriptures
Week 2	Understanding the Christian God as the Holy Trinity
Week 3	The Significance of Jesus being the Messiah
Week 4	The Significance of the Resurrection of Jesus
Week 5	The Holy Spirit and the New Testament
Week 6	Sin and Freedom through Jesus
Week 7	Why is Prayer and Encounter with God Important?

Week 8 Making Commitments to Discipleship and God's Blessing

So what has happened to those who were confirmed six months on? Of those who came from the Sunday Morning Parish Eucharist, most of the younger people are now regular participants coming up each week for Holy Communion, many of whom have taken an active part in the liturgy as servers and acolytes. Of the adults who were confirmed, again from those who attend the Parish Eucharist, most have committed to attending regular Sunday Services.

I am sad that many who came from the extended Nigerian, Sierra Leonean and West Indian families from the Sunday Eucharist Service have not become more active participants of the church. Many of these I think came because they saw it as a way to get into church schools and colleges. Of those who came via the church youth club, many have become active participants of the Sunday Morning Service. We have a long way to go to convert what is currently a youth club to become a youth fresh expression of church, which in time I hope will bring more candidates for baptism and confirmation. I am hopeful that as the New Monastic Community becomes more established, that there will be a growth in confirmations as well as lay and ordained vocations.

The challenge of keeping confirmation as a sacrament of belief and blessing rather than just as a means of accessing the education parents want for their children remains a big challenge. In the course we ran we stressed the importance of the commitments candidates were going to make, and that there has to be no pressure on them to 'have to do this'; it must be because of their own faith and free will. Only one young person withdrew from getting confirmed and that was because of the tension in her family situation of a Muslim father and a Christian mother.

I do not have any easy answers for how we approach the issue of parental pressure for access to schools, as I am sure that this is an issue that is not going to go away. However, I am now very convinced that confirmation is an important sacrament if we are serious about mission and discipleship in an age when we need to encourage a much deeper form of faith so that Christians have greater resilience in an increasingly complex world of consumerism and fundamentalism.

In the context of the North Peckham Estate, having the bishop as the point of unity with the diocese and an important leadership presence taking the sacrament of confirmation is so important. The people of North Peckham are used to being ignored by those of power and privilege. In an age when the divide between rich and poor grows ever wider, the presence of the bishop shows the Church to be a visible expression of the invisible kingdom of God, putting emphasis on God's preferential treatment and inclusion of the poor and those who are marginalized. In this celebration of the sacrament of confirmation, candidates are told their lives matter to the Church, and most of all that their lives matter to God, and that they are unconditionally loved and valued by God the Holy Trinity. This is so crucial for younger people continually being tested as they enter into the cut-throat market society we have created. Hopefully, through the confirmation course, we have laid some foundations for those who are young or who have only just encountered Christ, that through the sacraments of baptism and confirmation they may begin the journey of faith in obedience to Christ, receiving the love of a God in a world in which there isn't much love around. That those who have received confirmation encounter a Christ who desires all to flourish to their potential.

So to those who are reading this because they are mission-minded yet cynical about sacraments and in particular confirmation, I hope my experience will challenge you. Confirmation will never be a golden bullet to help us meet all the serious issues of Christian formation and initiation in the twenty-first century. However, I think it gives an opportunity for God to do what God will do. It creates a rare space and opportunity for the kingdom and the Church as a crucial staging post and blessing of those we seek to encourage to grow in faith and commitment to the way of Christ. If this not missional, then I don't know what mission is.

Let each of us accept the truth of the following statement and try to make it our most fundamental principle: Christ's teaching will never let us down, while worldly wisdom always will. Christ himself said that this sort of wisdom was like a house with nothing but sand as its foundation, while his own was like a building with solid rock as its foundation.[7]

Notes

1 As downloaded at https://churchpop.com/2016/03/05/lost-meaning-confirmation/.

2 'White Anglo-Saxon Protestant'.

3 Sisters of Notre Dame Chardon Ohio, *Confirmed in the Spirit Catechist Guide*, Loyola Press, Chicago, 2007.

4 Arthur Mason, *The Relation of Confirmation to Baptism: As Taught in Holy Scripture and the Fathers*, Longmans, Green, London, 1891; Dom Gregory Dix, *The Theology of Confirmation in Relation to Baptism*, 1946.

5 The sending of the people of God into the world to proclaim the gospel in word and action as central to God's mission in an age when in the Western world numbers of Christians diminishing.

6 Jeffrey John, *This Is Our Faith: A Popular Presentation of Church Teaching*, Redemptorist Publications, Chawton, 2014.

7 St Vincent de Paul, 1581–1660, in Frances Ryan and John E. Rybolt (eds), *Vincent de Paul and Louise de Mariliac: Rules, Conferences and Writings*, Paulist Press, Mahwah, 1995, p. 87.

PART 4

Sacraments in Eucharist and Holy Communion

For I received from the Lord what I also handed on to you, that the Lord Jesus on the night when he was betrayed took a loaf of bread, and when he had given thanks, he broke it and said, 'This is my body that is for you. Do this in remembrance of me.' In the same way he took the cup also, after supper, saying, 'This cup is the new covenant in my blood. Do this, as often as you drink it, in remembrance of me.' (1 Corinthians 11.23–25)

Introduction

Lucy Moore's Chapter 9 draws on research to explore how Holy Communion can be used in a context where people are non-churched, which is particularly challenging when the fresh expression includes adults and children. Lucy asks some astute questions which need to be faced in any new initiative shifting from mission to begin being an expression of church. There are no simple answers but Lucy shares important insights.

Karen Ward's Chapter 10 and Kim Hartshorne's Chapter 11 helpfully tell the story of a mission that grew into a fresh expression, and their stories open up how this process can happen. Do read Karen's seven really helpful summary points, which can be read not only for Communion but for most of the sacraments/sacramental, particularly working with the 'spiritual not religious'.

Kim's chapter gives real insights in a tough context, and her thoughts on contextualization are again very helpful for pioneers and missioners to reflect upon.

Finally Sue Wallace's Chapter 9 offers a realistic model and approach to the Eucharist as pilgrimage, which can be applied into lots of different contexts. This approach can provide a useful construct to navigate the shift from mission to church with a regular and contextual approach to Holy Communion or Eucharist.

9

Taste and See: Stories of How, When and Why Messy Churches Choose to Celebrate Holy Communion or Choose Not to

LUCY MOORE

The Messy Church team was delighted to be invited to take on the Easter Day main morning service – our first Messy Communion! The team spent Easter Saturday morning constructing a giant, cross-shaped table in the middle of our traditional church building, which was to act as the focal point for this special event.

From toddlers to senior citizens, regular church goers and Easter visitors, everyone joined in a range of activities which led us through Holy Week. The activities were interspersed between storytelling and hymns, when we all gathered back around the table in the centre of church. Palm crosses, shove ha'penny, word challenges (Jesus' teaching) and Gethsemane Garden cakes set the scene before we gathered for Communion. All ages took part in a most moving Communion service and shared freshly baked (gluten-free!) bread and grape juice. The celebration ended with Messy Grace and confetti cannons exploding over the congregation on the 'Amen'. Afterwards the children rushed outside for the annual Easter Egg Hunt in the churchyard and many people stayed for a tasty 'bring and share' lunch. Several people said that it wasn't what they had expected, but everyone seemed to enjoy the special Easter Messy Communion.

So writes Jenny Simmonds of Abbots Bromley. Her account highlights the way Messy Church teams, who often belong to both inherited and new forms of church, are bringing some of the Messy experience to enrich the traditional experience of Communion. We are at a time of change in the Church and need the gift of discernment and grace to know what of the old and new to cherish and nurture, and what we need to lose for the good of the kingdom and those not yet part of it. Communion sits at the heart of tradition and at the cutting edge of change.

We have a kitchen table, which we bought long ago. The table was where we ate as a family, gathered as friends and talked about the Bible together over strong coffee, baked successful bread and less edible scones, built with Duplo, created sticky masterpieces, wept over the death of a friend from alcoholism, glued autumn leaves on to posters, provided endless cups of tea to lonely churchwardens, argued over homework, fed children, adults, visitors from other countries, bishops and refugees; where we mended bikes and planned our move down south. Now its surface is scarred by small angry spoons and stained with the paint they said was washable. It tends to carry more glasses of wine than orange squash. The table is the silent witness to a lifetime of family breakfast, Bible time and prayer, of easy hospitality with friends and harder hospitality with strangers, of a network of friends around the world, of meals that ended with laughter or arguments, of endless conversations, of parties, of planning marvellous events for church, of family life lived in sticky, unhygienic, mysterious, robust, gently present reality.

As a focal point for healthy family life, it's little wonder that tables have a central place not just in homes but in many churches. Revd Mike Peatman described one Christmas Eve, when a man who had recently brought his family to a church meal knocked on his door and asked if he could borrow a table. His family had enjoyed the church meal so much that they wanted to sit around a table for their Christmas meal too, but they didn't own one. 'Take it!' said Mike. 'Keep it!' Mission by Gopak.

Gathering around a table gives a sense of belonging. It's hard to feel isolated – one of the curses of UK society – when you are elbow-to-elbow and face-to-face with fellow human beings. Indeed, it's hard not to be in a perpetual giggle when you realize that not only are you surrounded by human beings, but your very shoelaces are being tied together under the table by your six-year-old neighbour, as happened to me at a recent Messy tea.

There is also something human about gathering around a table piled high with a meal to share. Friends recently visited Micronesia on a church trip and were welcomed everywhere with tables groaning with local food. A well-filled table is a ceremonial symbol of welcome and hospitality, not just a way of stuffing bellies; it is part of being human and being more than just an individual. It creates community, it fosters belonging, it shouts out silently, 'You matter! You are worth it! You are one of us! We are together!'

It is this sense of belonging and shared humanity in the presence of a relational God that's at the heart of Messy Churches. Mark Woods writes:

> But evangelicalism has to ask itself whether it's entirely helpful to remove people's sense of belonging by confronting them with a choice they might not be ready to make. A binary, in-or-out, adversarial gospel is not always very appealing. Is it possible to combine warm inclusivity with a full-blooded call to repentance and faith? It won't be easy, but without that sort of theological and pastoral effort the Church will be increasingly sidelined from the mainstream of public life and thought.[1]

If belonging first – before behaving, believing and blessing – is turning out to be the pattern many families in Messy Churches follow as they walk together towards Christ; if belonging is so crucial to a discipleship journey; then what part does Holy Communion play in this journey? How does Communion help families feel they belong at that holy table? How does this two-thousand-year-old meal join together strangers and enemies within the family love of Christ and his Church and demonstrate to us all at the most profound level of our being that 'in [Christ] all things hold together' (Colossians 1.17)?

Is Communion a reward for the inner circle who have undergone a rite to demonstrate their commitment, or is it a means Jesus provided for anyone to taste and see that God is good, to experience for themselves the intimacy of relationship that comes through eating and drinking together, the reality of the bread and wine echoing the reality of God's unconditional love? Is it reserved for those who already believe or is it a means for those on their way to believing to grow in their belief? If the former, I would suggest we should probably avoid ever doing a Messy Communion: Messy Church is too open to outsiders, too outward-facing, too inclusive: there will be too many people excluded from the sacrament and it will become a measure of how divided we are rather than how united we are.

If the latter, we should probably try to have it more often, so that it becomes yet another means for anyone to encounter the love of God and for God to act in ways beyond our control. It won't amaze you to know that I'm more and more convinced that Communion is a mystery that Jesus has provided to help anyone come closer to him, including people with disabilities, people with different academic abilities, of different ages and levels of damage in their life experience, those nearer or closer to God. The more I learn from Christ in the stranger and the more I see him in people who have never been part of organized religion before, the more convinced I am that we are all so many gazillion miles away from understanding and appreciating what Communion really means that, as a Church, we should arguably simply make it available to everyone Jesus is drawing closer to him.

How many Messy Churches already do a Messy Communion? George Lings presented some of his research at the International Messy Church Conference in May 2016, from among Anglican fresh expressions (fxC). He says:

> When it comes to celebrating the sacraments the comparative picture is somewhat bleak; Messy Churches are the least

> likely to do either communions or baptisms, with only 12% doing the former and 21% doing the latter. The averages across other fxC are around 50%. I am aware that a short life history, being mainly lay led and drawing more non-churched people all play a part in this. In addition, the wider church is not sufficiently friendly to child communion or creative contextual liturgy for the non-churched and their families.[2]

It can take a long time to get to the place where a Messy Church feels it's right to gather around the Communion table. Communion may be a service of belonging, but with many Messy families only just starting to feel a sense of belonging to their church, sensitivity is needed to know at what point Communion puts a helpful shape on that sense of belonging, or when it is too early and would just reinforce the sense a family may have of being outsiders. There are so many variations in the regulations from church to church, that a Messy Church needs to plan clearly and communicate clearly who is welcome to do what in the service. There can be no assumption that everyone present believes in God or is baptized. Nor can it be assumed that because someone has been baptized, that they believe; or that they don't believe because they haven't been baptized. And children may feel much more strongly that this is their church and their God than parents or carers do. Little wonder that Messy Church, with its higher percentage of people with no church background than other forms of fxC, is taking longer to make the most of the God-given gift.

Many Messy Churches eventually feel the need to share Communion together, though as George points out, only a relative few have tried so far. Suggested sessions on Communion are provided in *Messy Church 2* and *Messy Church 3*[3] and when the magazine *Get Messy!*[4] had a session on the Last Supper, stories flooded in of Messy Communions being held. But we have not yet forcefully encouraged or resourced this approach because the core team members are all from middle-to-low churchmanship. As I write, however, a date has just been made for a Messy Liturgy Day for the Messy Church team and the

Liturgical Commission to try to make progress: this is a living story and there is goodwill on both sides to find a Godly way forward.

Two questions arise: What can Holy Communion do for Messy Church? What can Messy Church do for Communion? These sound utilitarian, but Messy Church has always had a strong element of the pragmatic.

What can Holy Communion do for Messy Church?

It would be surprising if Messy Churches weren't trying to hold Messy Communions. (Apart, that is, from the Salvation Army Messy Churches, who wouldn't be thinking about it for obvious reasons.) Look at the strong similarities between a Eucharist and a Messy Church session. Both have tables! Both gather around a meal at a key point in their liturgy; both rely not just on words but primarily on the senses and require something concrete and tangible in order to happen. Both expect people to participate, not remain as onlookers or spectators. Both have a strong focus on a story. Both try to build strong relationships – to build community: between Christ and his people, between one person and another, between different churches around the world and across time. They are both dramatic, involving actions as well as words – a script or structure, a shape that takes the participants on a journey. And at their best, they both demonstrate the Messy Church values of being Christ-centred, of hospitality and of celebration. I would find it hard to describe many of the Communion services I have attended in inherited church as 'creative' or 'all-age', however – the other two Messy Church values. More of these later.

So Communion can add an extra dimension to what is already going on in a Messy Church. It can be one of the factors that lifts it from the worst-case scenario of merely being a jolly family social fun time and give it a sense of the transcendent, the numinous, the unknowable: if Jesus came to bring 'life in all its fullness', one aspect of that might be indeed to help families appreciate the unknowable and to have windows opened to something way beyond cerebral understanding. It can be a time which draws the Messy Church together by looking at a person who is above and beyond and yet within their own circle. It can be a time of looking outwards to feel a connection with other churches, other Messy Churches also celebrating Communion in the same month . . . other congregations within their own local church . . . other churches within their denomination . . . indeed it can and should reinforce a connection with the whole global cross-history household of God.

And Communion can be a wonderful way to encourage the discipline of learning! My colleague Martyn Payne reflected on a visit he made to a Messy Church:

> And we broke bread together! It was the first time they had tried this and it was so good. Of course the theme was the Last Supper and so it was a natural part of the story that day. Just after the first course we paused and John described how Jesus took the bread at a meal just like this one and broke it and shared it so that they would remember him and what he did on the cross. We then all drank our specially prepared spiced blackcurrant juice! It was done so well and so reverently even in the midst of our messy mealtime. And it also sparked off lots of questions! Among the mums and children with whom I sat, it led to a conversation about believing in God and what Communion was all about. In other words, the faith sharing of Messy Church bubbled up during the mealtime as well and very naturally.

Possibly one of the most memorable conversations I have had was with Nicky, who came with her husband and children. They are regulars and in fact often also go to the other Messy Church at Eastgate in the town, which is a monthly. She was very down to earth and summarized the whole thing by saying, 'Isn't it good that we can learn about God in this sort of unlearny way'!

From another standpoint, Messy Church in a Catholic church Martyn visited has a similar but distinctive aim:

> They [the team] are very aware that many Catholic families simply come to the regular Mass but with little understanding of their faith outside the mystery of the Eucharist. For them Messy Church would therefore be an opportunity to help their existing congregation to engage creatively with the heart of what Christians believe. In other words, the evangelism or mission element of a Catholic Messy Church would primarily be internal discipleship, rather than looking particularly to reach brand new families from the community.

'Learning in an unlearny way', whatever stage on the journey we may be at: perhaps this is an opportunity the Eucharist can bring to Messy Church.

What can Messy Church do for Communion?

It's worth thinking about those five Messy Church values: being Christ-centred, creativity, all-age, celebration and hospitality. The Christ-centredness flows through everything.

In terms of creativity, some Communion services feel (and this may only be a perception but is nonetheless significant) prescribed and set in stone, all creativity exhausted years ago when the liturgy was written, and brought into being by and for a leader and group of people who have neither the permission, the confidence nor the desire to do anything except walk through the responses written for them. Any actor can tell you how fatally easy it is for a script to be killed by a lack of understanding or commitment to engage with it. The service is read, not known by heart. As a storyteller will tell you, knowing a story by heart would demonstrate that the teller cares enough about the story to have internalized it and made it part of them: a book just gets between the teller and the listener. A musician may take a score on stage. An actor doesn't. It cramps their communication, because their communication involves the visual and the kinaesthetic as well as the auditory. In the challenge of a Messy Church context, where there is little learned 'good behaviour' in the congregation (and anecdotal evidence suggests most 'inappropriate behaviour' comes from adults rather than children!), powerful communication is crucial and every creative resource is needed to share the 'story' effectively. Reading from a book won't cut the mustard. The story is worth more than that. Messy Church gives the challenge of sharing the story with fresh creativity with a new generation.

As for being 'all-age', although more children are welcome in services than used to be the case, Communion tends to be still a service by adults, for adults, in adult language, to suit adult preferences for mobility and with more 'don'ts' than 'dos', more restriction than invitation, more work at the people than work of the people. So one aspect of the mutual give and take of Messy Church is a new imperative to communicate this ancient sacrament in an effective way for all God's people, not just the grown-ups. Half of a Messy Church is made up of children: the Church has the opportunity for children as well as adults to fall in love with this ancient ritual and make Jesus' story their story too. Perhaps as Messy Church leaders creatively work out how to share that story with all ages, some of the creativity around language, actions and the senses will osmose into inherited church too, breathing new life into dry bones.

The value of Celebration means there is a sense of wanting Communion to share that Spirit-filled joy, so present in Messy Churches. While it is not incongruous to have silence and moments of awe, the joyless dullness and boredom I experienced in Communion services through my childhood are certainly incongruous there. We are offered the chance to remember joy within the solemnity of the service.

With a core value of 'hospitality', belonging is at the heart of what we're trying to do in Messy Church. We want people to be able to say with integrity and excitement, 'This is our church. This is our God. This is our story. This is our family. This is where we feel at home, accepted, known by name and free to take risks because we know that here we are most deeply loved.' If Messy Church can help some churches, as well as 'Messy guests' rediscover that sense of genuine belonging together around God's table, that is a great gift to share.

The Book of Common Prayer insists that a 'fair white Linen cloth' covers the table, and that it stands 'in the body of the Church'. Messy Church tables may be covered with pvc wipe-clean cloths rather than linen, but they stand in the same tradition, firmly in the body of the church, in among the people, not reserved for the 'deserving few' at set times of year. Both ancient and Messy are trying to help people encounter the holiness of a God beyond our human understanding through the hospitable Christ who welcomes all who are hungry and thirsty, whatever their age, to the table of the King.

Notes

1 www.christiantoday.com/article/church.decline.is.evangelicalism.to.blame/76962.htm.

2 Keynote Talk at Messy Church International Conference, May 2016.

3 Lucy Moore, *Messy Church 2: Ideas for Discipling a Christ-Centred Community*, Messy Church, Oxford, 2012; Lucy Moore, *Messy Church 3: Fifteen Sessions for Exploring the Christian Life with Families*, Messy Church, Oxford, 2012.

4 *Get Messy!* is a four-monthly subscription resource for Messy Church leaders, Messy Church, Oxford.

10

Developing the Sacramentality of Holy Communion as the Orientation of the Heart

KAREN WARD

Many Europeans assume that the United States is predominantly a 'churched country', so that the emphasis then for starting any mission pursuit on this side of the pond begins with the 'de-churched'. This assumption is a stereotype as, on the West and East coasts of the USA, there are a rising number of the 'never-churched', people whose parents were part of an original cohort who left churches of all denominations starting with the carnage of the First and Second World Wars and increasing until today. A good example of this is the Fremont area of Seattle. The City of Seattle in the State of Washington is one of the most 'de-and-unchurched' places in the USA, and the area of Fremont an example of even fewer Christians and churchgoers. In fact Fremont had only one remaining church before Church of the Apostles was founded there. The neighbourhood had been the centre of arts in the city for many decades and maintains the motto 'Libertas Quirkas' (the freedom to be different, 'free' thinking, acting and non-conformist). The local arts council issues 'passports' to artists from 'The People's Republic of Fremont'. A massive, soviet-built statue of Vladimir Lenin sits in the public square as an 'art piece', which is decked with 'holiday lights' each December.

After many years working at the churchwide office of the Evangelical Lutheran Church of America (ELCA), in Chicago, I felt called to pioneer a new expression of church among my non-churchgoing friends in Chicago. I met a Lutheran bishop in Seattle who was interested in reaching out to 'Gen Xers' in post-grunge Seattle, so I took up his offer, quit my job at the denominational headquarters in Chicago and moved to Seattle to begin this work. Fremont is known as an artistic and creative part of town, inhabited by many who are termed 'hipsters', regarding religion as the 'spiritual not religious', or what I heard someone say as 'ABC', 'Anything But the Church'. I felt drawn to Fremont, moving from my long-time home in Chicago, because I sensed that the Holy Spirit was very present in the lives of many who were seeking for significance and transformative experience, but assumed that this was not to be found in Christianity and definitively not in church.

So looking back at it now, I followed what Ian and Phil have identified in the circle diagram in the Introduction of this book, p. xvi. I spent a lot of time walking around and meeting people, joining in with events, and watching and listening to God in the context of Fremont. After a while we began a gathering in a local beer bar to discuss spirituality and theology. This seemed like a great place to reach out to both the de-and-unchurched of Fremont, and it quickly grew from a form of event, to a gathering of a group of faithful followers as an early stage form of community. So for a while we built this proto-community through gatherings for discussions in pubs, and as the relationships between people grew, we began to meet in people's homes. This then moved people from exploring general questions of spirituality, to questions specifically around Christianity as people began to trust and open up to those in the group. This began the journey from enquirer to disciple. Vitally, much of this was dependent on not forcing people to do things they did not want to do, and also to wait for people to ask the deep questions on their hearts when they were ready to be asked, and not push this. We remember that mission is God's not ours, so there is a missional discipline to wait for the Holy Spirit to unsettle people to ask existential and religious questions when they are ready.

So thinking about pioneering, I can see now with the wisdom of hindsight, that people began with questions around thinking and the head, but were actually seeking significance and transformational experience that can't be met through a discussion group, Bible study or fellowship. The breakthrough came through the experience of sacrament. I cannot now quite remember exactly why, but the issue of religious services began after people started in home groups, who then asked 'why we did not do religious services for irreligious people' It seemed that people were reaching out to seek to express the religious and spiritual journey they were on, which then felt for them a way of doing some form of worship service that they were comfortable with, and further, that they felt there was something special and spiritually significant about 'Holy Communion'.

However, it became clear very early on that we could not use some form of inaccessible liturgy using language they did not understand in a building that felt alien (as many church spaces felt for many at this time). No, we felt called to set up a spiritual community mission in a shopfront in mid-Fremont, in what then came across as safe public space, which would then act as a hub and gathering place as a teashop, meeting space, art space, and worship space with a flat above for guests to come and stay. So the Church of the Apostles was born as an unusual mission of an ecumenical partnership between the Episcopal Church of the United States and the ELCA, with a generous grant for mission development from Trinity Wall Street and other donors. So we began the building of a staff team as well as a missional community. Instead of dumbing down or creating 'liturgy-lite' services, there was an interest and positive enthusiasm for looking at some of the more ancient expressions of liturgy in the Church, and many of these resonated deeply not only with the de-churched, but somehow because these things were old, held a mystical intrigue for those who were coming from a 'spiritual not religious' unchurched perspective.

So we began with a Service of Holy Communion where we played with chants by writing original music and worked with authorized texts from our two mother church denominations, and somehow the mystery of bread and wine became the medium for spiritual encounter with God, with those gathered including the 'de-and-unchurched', which was unexpected. In the West, so much emphasis is still placed on thinking and understanding – as a faith pursuit of the orientation of the mind, that we often neglect the importance of faith experience as the orientation of the heart through sacrament that begins with the mysterious presence of Jesus in Holy Communion. In a world now defined by consumer experience, we again need to engage in mission of Word and sacrament, of thinking, learning and experiencing the love of God, to enable people to find faith, as well as deepen it. The importance then of sacrament as the orientation and experience of the heart as part of a conversion experience cannot be overestimated. We forget that just experiencing Christ's presence in Bread and Wine shared can be a converting ordinance. I have a number of friends who are now ordained priests where this conversion through experience of God through sacrament happened in a totally unexpected way.

The experience of Holy Communion was so deeply valued by my little emerging church mission, that services became weekly on Saturdays because this was when people had more time to meet. So as I tell this story, what can I unpack for those pioneers who are seeking to develop a Holy Communion sacramentality in a missional community? Here are my thoughts.

Sacramentality is birthed out of creativity

There is a connection between encouraging creativity in how we do mission, community and worship, with the beginnings of a sacramentality. Some of this is well known around ritual action, such as writing down the things that 'take your life away' using water-based ink, to watch these words being lifted off the page when they are put in water as an expression of repentance and forgiveness. Or dropping stones into water as a form of prayer as a metaphor for giving up whatever is burdening you to God. The list is endless. Such ritual actions can be added as a response activity to a spirituality discussion group, and equally the beginnings of a time of worship as community forms and people seek to make some form of spiritual expression which might not yet be fully Christian. Using creativity connected to some form of ritual response then becomes a space for people to encounter God through some form of symbolic action. When a community shifts to having a specifically Christian focus, then not only can the elements of bread and wine be introduced, but they can then be linked to creative readings of the gospel texts of Jesus, the disciples and the last supper. In this form, the sacrament of bread and wine then is given room for God to be made present to those gathered in ways we often do not comprehend, as people experience Jesus and the Holy Trinity to be true through such remembering and ritual action. Finally, the aesthetic of the space of worship needs consideration. This is not to manipulate people, but more about taking seriously how the sacred is made present in ordinary places. So in Church of the Apostles we had a young painter who had never painted icons before, who through photos of ancient images such as Rublev's ikon of the Trinity, fashioned large versions painted on plywood. Yes, we utilized candles, and at times incense to encourage the context as a place of awe, of mystery and of encounter with God. The use then of creative ritual action helped many to shift from thinking about Christianity to experiencing the Christian God, helping the community to move from forming community to developing discipleship, where developing discipleship was not just about people becoming Christian or restoring faith through thinking, but also about creating the opportunity for people to experience God through forms of ritual action as sacramental worship, to experience God through the heart. This was a crucial step then for the unchurched exploring faith to experience the reality of God's love for them, and for the de-churched to reconstruct and shift from head to heart to get beyond doubt and cynicism to again experience God as a reality beyond words and simple constructions of faith.

Sacramentality begins when real community is established, where people are prepared to be open and vulnerable to each other and God

As the circle diagram in the Introduction of this book expresses, it is important not to start with forms of worship service if you are truly committed to mission otherwise you are in great danger of collecting Christians from other churches. If I had not spent a considerable amount of time listening to context, and starting with some form of spiritual discussion group focused on those who not members of any church, then the sacramentality would not have been missional or contextual, as it would have been an expression of me and a few who gathered to support me. So the journey from loving action to forms of community to then exploring shared spiritual expression should not be rushed. People need time to break down negative stereotypes about Christians, the Christian faith and the Church, to then begin to build relationships of integrity and then and only then will they start to open up and choose to expose who they really are, and the deep questions and issues they travel with. This is not only a deeply relational process of building trust, I also believe there is something of the Holy Spirit unsettling people to seek and explore the spiritual which again needs great sensitivity. This unsettling activity of the Holy Spirit is again beyond words, and is the beginning of a yearning for the sacred as the beginning of a sacramentality.

Sacramentality develops when enough attention is given to context to express the inexpressible

My friends Jonny Baker of Church Mission Society (CMS) fame, and Mark Pierson, a missional Baptist minister from New Zealand, talk about the importance of the pioneer and skills in worship curation.[1] This competency is as important as the ability to curate a modern art gallery. The skill is how to enable liturgy and sacrament to be fully experienced through some form of event or worship service. The words of expression need to be authentic, contextual and metaphorical. A good example are the Christian and patriarchal words we use for the Holy Trinity. For some difficult relationships with parents particularly, 'fathers' can be in some contexts an obstacle to experiencing God, while for others the specifically male exclusive language of God prevents those passionate about gender-inclusiveness from understanding and experiencing God positively. So, in response, we sometimes talk of God the Creator, God the Redeemer and God the Sustainer as metaphorical language to express some of the biblical truths of the Christian and biblical understandings of God.[2] Also this act of worship curation needs a thought about what art, what words are meaningful in context. A good example was a service we held on an Easter Sunday one year, when we invited local street artists to help make a contemporary Reredos (an ancient screen in three parts placed behind an altar). Not only did this create a contextual aesthetic but encouraged those who had created the art to take part in the service, where some who had become Christian through our mission activities were baptized using beer barrels (again contextual) with the high point of the service, celebrating the resurrection through the presence of Christ through the receiving of Christ through bread and wine. This whole service could have been an unprecedented disaster if we had not curated it well, and given room for a form of contemporary liturgy that held the various activities together, and opened up the importance of the bread and wine as an ongoing spiritual gift to sustain us.

Sacramentality begins in the unsettling of the Holy Spirit in people's lives

In many of the books and teaching on mission and fresh expressions of church it is often quoted that mission is about 'catching up with what God is already doing'.[3] Not only is this a positive understanding of God's work in the details of our lives, but it is also a truth repeated in 2 Corinthians chapter 5 that God is restoring all things back into right relationship with God, and then this is the scary thing, through us. Literally as we are friends with God, so we call others to be reconciled and friends with God also. Now bad theology and mission practice here would say that we somehow speak on behalf of an absent God, so must 'win people for the kingdom' in some form of commercial sales pitch or training course. This I think can be very damaging and an unhelpful way of understanding God's mission through us. Instead I think we are called to 'prayerful action', which is about seeking the wisdom to understand what God is doing in people's lives, to then be sensitive and encouraging as they explore the reality of God through their own experience and understanding. We must not push people hard, we are called rather to be enablers to help people explore faith on their terms. As I have already said, I think the Holy Spirit is often more of an irritant or unsettler of people, to help them reach beyond secure and narrow thinking, to explore the faith more fully. As I heard an Evangelist once say, 'you never force a baby to eat against its will, no you feed a baby when it expresses its hunger through crying'. Likewise we are called to support people and their explorations and their questions when they ask them rather than trying to make them feel guilty or somehow trying to force them to face spiritual questions when they are not ready to do so. This discipline of prayerful waiting is extremely difficult and requires infinite patience. However, this process of unsettling of the Holy Spirit needs to be fed in two ways – thinking with the head and experience with the heart. This unsettling then is a form of conversion for both those who are not yet Christian and for those going deeper with Christianity – to find faith, and to go deeper with following Jesus, in the mystery and encounter with God through Word (teaching and knowledge) and sacrament (the experience of God through ritual action and symbol encourages encounter with God and wisdom). The two go hand in hand, and we must remember we often have no idea what God is doing and communicating with people through God the Holy Spirit.

Sacramentality develops when you dig deep within church liturgical tradition

It might sound crazy, but as the community of Church of the Apostles grew, one of the groups that was most supported was what we called a 'liturgy guild'. Anyone could join this group, which was responsible for exploring, finding and contextualizing very ancient forms of liturgy, and taking the words of ancient chants and setting them in forms of contemporary music. In this way liturgy and sacramental worship and spiritual expression became part of a living tradition, where we explored two thousand years of resources in the Western and Eastern Christian Churches. Liturgy then becomes 'the work of the people', and opens up those who are either exploring or new to the faith to ancient traditions that express the struggles, successes, pain and joy of the people of God to and with God the Holy Trinity. This ancient depth then emphasizes and reinforces the importance of sacrament with the focus on Holy Communion as it has been expressed over the ages. This opening up people to the historic sense of a continuing tradition helps those exploring Christianity from a 'spiritual not religious' perspective and also those who had been de-churched from more 'fundamentalist' expressions of church with a narrow view of theology and practice. The liturgy guild took ancient resources and explored how they could be used in contemporary expressions of worship, and in so doing, deepened an appreciation of Holy Communion as spiritual experience which in turn opened up deeper understandings of theology and the depth of the Christian faith.

Sacramentality begins when people are open to experience Jesus as the ultimate source of love

We often forget it, but ultimately love cannot be fully understood with the head but needs to be experienced with the heart. If the ancient Mothers and Fathers of the Church are correct, then fundamentally Christianity can only be fully lived when we have experienced God's love for us. For some who are fortunate, they experience this Grace of God's unconditional love as part of their conversion or restorative experience. Unfortunately, for many this experience of God's love as part of their 'becoming Christian' was not their experience. Yes we can have spiritual experiences from reading Scripture, from singing hymns, songs, choruses and chants – but ultimately I think it is God's blessing through the sacraments that is often the means by which God bestows love to and on us. The regular sacrament of Holy Communion then needs to play its part in sustaining and providing the space for God to mediate the love of the Holy Trinity to and with us through sacramental liturgy, sign and symbol. Without the love of God and the experience of this love, the Christian life is a very difficult path to follow if it is only in our minds and strength. As we remember in the New Commandment, to love the Lord our God with your heart, mind and strength, and love your neighbour as yourself, can only be truly sustained if it is nourished by the receiving of God's love – so regular receiving of the sacrament of Holy Communion is vital as part of this ongoing nourishment of God's love for us.

Sacramentality works when we allow God to be in control and allow for spontaneity

The great difference between sacramental tradition and sacramental traditionalism is the issue of control. For some the emphasis of sacramental worship is that we must keep everything the same and impose it on context, even when it is anachronistic or uses words and symbols that are alien or not understood. This I believe defines traditionalism as almost a form of sacramental institutionalization. As all pioneers and missioners know, everything has to be contextualized and opened up, and be the 'work of the people' if it is to be relevant and effective. The language, ritual action and symbol need to be opened up, or more precisely, freed up. The liturgy of Holy Communion can be expressed like a jazz band. Yes there is an order, there is a starting place, a middle and an end, but this needs to be God breathed. So taking in the insights of worship curation and the place of the Holy Spirit in sacramental expressions of worship – the space for forms of individual response as spontaneity is important. This could be done through making some form of art, prayer stations, using a labyrinth, using Godly Play, using a form of *Lectio Divina* (for people to explore the Gospel reading in the run-up to receiving Communion); in fact there are infinite ways of giving space for the spontaneous spiritual expression and encounter. This I think helps keep the focus then on spiritual experience, avoiding the downsides of liturgical and sacramental institutionalization. This requires a certain amount of considered risk-taking and living with the consequences when things are not as great as we would want. However, such creative spontaneity does activate the community to fully participate and therefore, we hope, experience God.

One of the greatest risks I think we have in doing mission seeking to form new Christians and restore those who have lost their faith, is to place too much emphasis on thinking and learning with the heads. The great danger then can be that everything ends up being about thinking. In my experience of some forms of alternative worship, it can end up more about a thinking workshop about God rather than a form of worship as a space to express love to God in community and to receive the love of God. Sacrament, and in particular Holy Communion, then becomes an important counter to this, to ensure that there is an emphasis on experiencing God with the heart that gets beyond thinking, and if we are committed to the path of spiritual transformation, then we need an approach of both head and heart, of knowing and experiencing God, that takes people much deeper into faith and discipleship. Without sacraments this would be impossible, and so the task of the pioneer or missioner who has successfully started a mission project engaging with 'de-and-unchurched' people is to begin the process of developing a sacramentality, beginning with creativity and ritual action that then becomes fully expressed in the sacraments and ultimately sustained through the regular receiving of Holy Communion. Developing this sacramentality helps a fresh expressions project shift from being a mission, to becoming a missional ecclesial community, an expression of church.

So what happened to the Church of the Apostles? Well with these sacramental considerations in place it grew from being a mission to being a mission church with the DNA of a New Monastic Community. In time it moved from the shopfront tea-shop to rehabilitate an old empty Lutheran Church just across the street to open up Fremont Abbey, which became a hub for music, the arts and the expression of Christian spirituality. Now well established, they no longer needed me as a founding ordained priest, so I have left and I am now pioneering and seeking to create a new missional community in connection with a poor Episcopalian Parish Church in Portland Oregon, using these same insights regarding sacramentality to reinvigorate a parish church into a healthy missional community we are calling 'Portland Abbey'.

So how does this commitment to a process of sacramentality begin? Well I think this begins with the faith and risk of a pioneer or pioneering group who is/are not afraid of beginning and facing the spiritual process that leads a community to develop the sacramental signs of becoming a missional church. I am reminded of the words of Martin Luther King Jr, one of my teachers when he said: 'Take the first step in faith. You don't have to see the whole staircase, just take the first step.'[4]

Amen to that!

Notes

1 See https://canterburypress.hymnsam.co.uk/books/9781848251946/the-art-of-curating-worship and www.churchpublishing.org/curatingworship.

2 For more information on this explore work of Sallie McFague and her previous name of Sallie TeSelle.

3 S. Croft and I. Mobsby (eds), *Ancient Faith Future Mission: Fresh Expressions 1, the Sacramental Tradition*, Canterbury Press, Norwich, 2012, p. 61.

4 http://stjameswilkinsburg.org/martin-luther-king-jr-quotes-on-faith-and-god/.

11

Communion and the Story of the Upper Room

KIM HARTSHORNE

Introduction

In this chapter, I hope to tell the story of how one new church community found more and deeper meaning in the Eucharist. By walking with people who were totally 'unchurched', the leaders of the group – a few long-standing but somewhat battered Christians from evangelical and charismatic backgrounds – were led into new encounters with God through sharing bread and wine, seeing through the eyes of others the beauty of grace and belonging being offered at the Table.

Background

The Upper Room Community began eight years ago as a safe place for people who were far away from church to begin to explore faith, and see what a life of faith might look like lived out up close. We began offering two drop-in sessions a week in a rented office above shops in a small market town with a significant amount of unseen deprivation. Through word of mouth people began to come along. At the drop-in, we listen to people who do not have others to talk to, and we drink tea. We offer prayer, hang out together, celebrate birthdays, eat meals together and go for trips out. There are many reasons people come along: they live alone and feel isolated; they are disabled or live with long-term physical or mental ill health conditions and want relief; they are stressed and struggling with debt or family problems. Some are looking for friendship, a safe place and some people to chat to, others want specific help writing a letter or fighting a case, or help and support for a child in the education system. Most people are looking for belonging; a community of safe people to journey through the ups and downs of life with.

Worship

Our worshipping life has developed in recent years within the framework of the Church of England, as I have trained as an ordained pioneer minister and the Upper Room has been designated a Bishops Mission Order. This process of emerging into a new denominational partnership has shaped our worshipping identity and given us additional guidelines to work within, a long tradition to access and inhabit, and the concept of authorized liturgy to push against and wrestle with. We have worked to discover ways in which we can enter into our new identity with integrity, create accessible and culturally appropriate rituals for a very diverse and complex community, but which are also cognisant with and recognizable as part of the family of the Church of England. This journey has brought us into a much deeper engagement with the theology and meaning of the Eucharist.

Prior to this, our leaders were mainly from church backgrounds that considered Communion 'just a memorial', that was re-enacted every now and again with little in the way of reverence or expectation. Our journey with others, and the tradition we have entered into, has opened up to us new and blessed depths that were unavailable to us before. Over the course of this journey we have been transformed from identity as a 'project' or charity into becoming church, a full part of the body of Christ.

In the Jewish apocalyptic tradition, re-telling and re-enacting a story from the past enables it to come alive again in the fresh telling, presenting itself each time as a present participation, and so the sense of remembered events enters into the present and ruptures our familiarity, becoming a live meeting place with the living God in the bread and wine. Dunn speaks of this tradition as reminding us of our identity through the re-enactment of hope;[1]

each time we participate together in the Eucharist – rehearsing our forgiveness from sin, our cleansing, our sharing in the peace of Christ, our remembering the love and service Jesus showed his friends, the invitation of the left out to the feast, and the sharing in the brokenness of Christ's body for us – we remind ourselves of our salvation, our restoration and our resurrection, and become formed into our saviour's story a little more.

Access and inculturation

It's important to consider the social and cultural barriers that church presents for people with physical impairment, mental health difficulties or learning disabilities – so much of our standard liturgical life as Anglicans is based on being able to read, process, follow, and requires significant mobility for standing up, sitting down, kneeling and queuing. If you are new to church, with no background of attendance, it can be incredibly difficult to pick up what is going on, and hard to have any idea what any of it means or how it could relate to your daily life. People tell us they feel uncomfortable, as if they 'don't fit in'. They feel more relaxed in a homely space with fewer people and a simpler means of worship. When I asked one young man how he felt when he visited a larger local church, he said: 'People kept looking at me all the time. I thought I must've been doing something wrong.'

This could say as much about the lack of social and cultural diversity in some of our local congregations in a predominantly white, middle-class, middle-aged, local demographic, but for all of us, feeling safe and comfortable are usually prerequisite to opening ourselves up to new things. People coming to the Upper Room over the years have suffered abuse, trauma, violation, bullying, life-limiting illness or disability, debt or intervention by Social Services in their lives. Due to the trauma or shame of these life events, people often say they don't like to be looked at or seen by others. They seek safety and comfort, and so gravitate to a smaller space where they can get to know a smaller number of people well.

Over the years we have worked to strip back and simplify the language, locations, rituals and practices of Christian faith, to mix up who leads and speaks, and to 'de-clutter' what is happening in Communion, to reduce the cultural hurdles. We meet in a room with sofas and armchairs; everyone is seated in a circle at the same level and remain seated throughout; there is no lectern; a simpler translation of the Bible is used, following the lectionary; people who are new to the group are asked to join in by offering the cup of grape juice or writing prayers. Over time, we have seen people come along, join in, and begin to ponder on the meaning and how it relates to their own lives. It has been a long, slow mutual process, entering into one another's culture in order to understand something of life there, listening and joining in, in order to weave together the message of the gospel and share in it together, gaining mutual understanding. St Paul perhaps spoke of this when he said 'I have become all things to all people' in the Bible (1 Corinthians 9.19–23); Jesus coming from heaven to become human is surely the ultimate act of inculturation!

It is an important way of working for us and it means that sharing the gospel is a two-way process, where we learn from one another where God might be at work and in what ways. There is an inherent vulnerability in this process for all, as in opening ourselves to another's culture and being invited into it as a guest, we must lower our guard and be open to new perspectives and ways of seeing. The host culture must open itself to a new person with new views and experiences, and if this is not to turn into a cultural boxing match of point scoring, then laying down certainties must occur in each party. There is mutual sharing and accepting that we all hold different pieces of the jigsaw puzzle, we all have experiences to share that are valuable, and that may open up gaps in the clouds for us all to glimpse God at work, shining through the lives of others.

Confessing and accepting our weakness

Learning to journey with people who have suffered violation or impairment has caused us to become more truthful about our own weakness and limitations, and eventually to cease presenting only a victorious Christ in our catechesis. We have been led by the people who come to consider the deep solidarity of Christ with our own rejection, pain and woundedness. This has deepened trust in the community as we are all enabled to speak the truth of our damage more openly. Eiesland draws attention to Christ's wounded body as one who calls disciples to

> recognize in the marks of impairment their own connection with God and their own salvation. In doing so, the [disabled] God is the revealer of a new humanity . . . the revelation of true personhood. Our bodies participate in the *Imago Dei* in and through . . . impairments and not despite them.[2]

She makes the point that humans are all vulnerable and share the same need for welcome; if we deny this common need and categorize people by disability or impairment, we deny and devalue all humanity, including our own.

Reynolds also highlights the tendency in Christian circles to assume that physical healing and restoration from impairment must be goals of our Christian life, predicated on the idea of perfection at Creation. This presents suffering as always a problem to be solved 'rather than sympathetically and redemptively encountered'.[3] Among Christians seeking to volunteer at the drop-in, this underpinning assumption has at times engendered a desire for activism, solutions, positivity and the need to find a theological 'explanation' for the sufferings of another, all of which can be most unhelpful. We let people self-identify their difficulties and solutions as much as possible and respond to their lead in their approach to them.

Reynolds shows a person not as a problem to be solved but

> a presence whose call for affirmation elicits a moral obligation to listen and pay attention, to show compassion that reflects back their distinct creaturely beauty and value . . .

> The real task is to be present to others, and this requires moral skills gained in relationships of interdependence and not in cognitive propositions.[4]

It would be fair to say that we have been led to a much deeper understanding of our own humanity and our faith as made manifest in the physical, limited body, as we journey with people whose bodies have been impacted by suffering.

It also occurs to me that much of our religious language around sin assumes it is *all* personal, and we are to blame for all of it. There is not, however, a clear line between being a sinner, and living with the consequences of being sinned against. The people we meet are often those who have been survivors of institutional or intergenerational sin and injustice. Many are living with the pain and disconnectedness of being sinned against. The process of coming to understand and accept that you are a beloved child of God, and how to order your life to live in the truth of that, is a lifetime's journey for many. Simply surviving, and mitigating pain, is a strong impulse that can lead people down roads of self-destruction. As yet I have seen no liturgy of confession or absolution that acknowledges this complexity, and offers the love and grace of God instead of condemnation. Our concept of confession and absolution, what restoration looks like, needs to broaden out, to admit the complexity of sin and how it manifests itself in broken lives. These are some of the issues we wrestle with in using authorized words for preparation and confession; where they are not nuanced enough we write alternatives or allow open space for people to confess in their hearts.

Non-verbal communication: the peace

Some people may have little formal education but our church is very warm in its care, shown when the community shares 'the Peace' during a Eucharist service. Despite damage, impairment and often verbal limitations, people's bodies communicate love during our monthly Eucharist service. Several older women always kiss me on the mouth at times of greeting and during the Peace. Although this crosses a personal boundary for me, I have learned to see it as a sign of mutual belonging, in the context of a ritual of love and belonging. It is a moment when the community comes together, up close and personal, and we are opened up to the fullness of belonging to one another, with all our weaknesses, hygiene issues or desperate loneliness.

Jean Vanier speaks of his experience living with people with learning difficulties of the need to listen to the

> non-verbal language of the body . . . some people can only talk with their bodies; only from there do true words flow. Sometimes . . . they cannot speak, but it may also be because they have lost trust in words.[5]

This prolonged period of hugging and handshaking is a time where non-verbal language can be spoken in many ways. It is a small glimpse into a wider process of listening to one another's bodies that occurs during the drop-in and other times, and can then be woven into our practices as we learn of one another.

Vanier draws a parallel with the tower of Babel, explaining that as disciples we need to 'learn the language of the other . . . in their own culture; their ways of eating . . . interacting, their ways of doing things, their forms of relationships [and] you will begin to discover the secret of communion'.[6] He describes this learning the ways of others as 'engendering meaning and hope, gradually restoring a broken self-image . . . through a caring committed presence, people discover that they are loved and so are lovable'.[7] As leaders, we have learned to listen and read the non-verbal communications of bodies that have suffered and not been heard, and to let each person lead the journey of finding meaning in their own bodily suffering.

Elisabeth Moltmann-Wendel describes Jesus' healing by touch as a significant time of communication to the self found in the body.[8] She describes mutual exchanges of touching that took place between the sick and excluded, in which Jesus also receives care and affirmation. She explains the use of the Greek word *haptein* in Jesus' healing encounters as an everyday word for touching, not related to the ritualized laying on of hands.[9] It is the word used when Jesus touches lepers in Mark 1.41; children in Mark 10.13; disciples in Matthew 17.7, when the bleeding woman touches Jesus, and when the woman anoints his feet in Luke 7.38. It describes a natural, mutual contact. She asserts Jesus' touch 'gave people confirmation for their existence . . . to touch means to stimulate people in their whole existence . . . to heal their brokenness and make them once again capable of contact, thought, experience'.[10]

This ministry of touching, which communicates non-verbally, stands over against much modern church practice, from the long apologetics lectures presented by Nicky Gumbel in the Alpha course, to the long and wordy liturgies of the authorized Anglican and Roman Catholic rites. There is an underlying and complex set of assumptions about words, their effectiveness, meaning and accessibility, which is not borne out when working among people who are educationally disadvantaged. The *Faith in the City Report* identified this two decades ago and perhaps little has changed:

> Status in the Christian community has tended to be seen as a consequence of academic study. The Catechism was traditionally something to be 'learnt' . . . and the building up of a Christian community was promoted primarily by education and study. All this has greatly favoured the life of the Church among people of above average literacy and intellectual ability; it has accorded well with the education, the reading habits and the social conventions of the upper and middle classes. But it has always been an obstacle to nurturing the Church in a working class environment . . . There is no obvious necessity to give this kind of thinking priority over other means of communication which God may use to stir our imagination.[12]

Participation

Anglicans recognize the Eucharist as a sacrament and a rite of participation on the journey of faith that allows new believers to appropriate the metaphors of new life into their own lives and bodies. It is hugely important that this is a participatory ritual, drawing us into belonging in the body of Christ on equal terms.

This has an impact on who leads, who discusses the Bible passage, who prays – in short, the whole community participates, so that we see the truth of our equal unworthiness and equal invitation to the Table woven throughout the service. My journey of learning to inhabit priesthood in this setting has been a radically different journey at the Upper Room than in a parish, because roles and expectations of the priest among those who are 'un-parished' are very different. I am able to experiment and ask for much greater participation in the roles and practices that are usually assumed to belong to the priest, with a sense that so long as I am present and holding the space then I can ask others to distribute the bread and wine, or say parts of the eucharistic prayer.

There is a levelling in the eucharistic ritual that reminds us all of the radically inclusive table fellowship of Christ on earth, and the levelling, unifying need for all humans to eat food and be in community in order to flourish. Jesus instituted a ritual that would connect humans to our weakness and vulnerability, to one another, and to his welcome and gathering in of the excluded at the great eschatological banquet of Luke 14.15–24.

Eating together at the Eucharist became a symbol of our 'togetherness' and as we came before God in our weakness, we became bound together as a people who saw one another deeply, and this sharing and interchange increased our commitment to be a people of truth and vulnerability. It has become a ritual in which we unmask and choose to reveal our hidden and fragile selves, and is often a vale of tears as we see ourselves and others through the astounding love of Christ. We always eat a meal together after Communion now as a way of cementing the communal practice of eating together.

When I asked others about what joining in at Communion means for them, one young man who always wants a role in the service said: 'We get to join in and be part of the team. We are together, we do this together. I feel a part of things when I have a job to do.'

Love, bread and mystery

There is one further aspect of the Eucharist and its connection to eating and the body that has emerged among us. Angel Méndez-Montoya writes of the love that is expressed when one prepares food for others whom God loves. He describes a process of 'alimentation', nourishment for body and soul which is transformative to the giver and recipient whereby both meet with God; he describes being nourished as 'being in the care of the cosmos . . . and of Divine care . . . eating together is a "mediating act"',[13] which combines traditions around food with new possibilities for experimentation and creativity, akin to an inculturated culinary liturgy.

People who come to the Upper Room express delight at eating together but several admitted they couldn't cook and only ate food out of tins with a spoon or packets of biscuits at home. This seemed to denigrate the dignity of humans and as a result a basic cooking class was set up in which people learn to handle ingredients, taste and smell, chop and stir and knead bread, as a way of connecting the somatic experience of food with making positive choices about health and self-care.

Méndez-Montoya concludes that the practices of cooking and eating in community are extensions of the gathering and hospitality that is intensified in the Eucharist. Examining participation in acts necessary to our common humanity, such as cooking and eating, introduces people to experiencing the divine, showing us a 'dimension of immanent practice and . . . new ways of bringing about individual and social transformation' that reflects a 'divine transcendental sharing . . . intensif[ying] immanence'.[14]

He explains a process of exchange between communal eating and participation in the Eucharist in which both inform the other; the communal meal increases awareness of culture and material practice brought into the eucharistic ritual over time, and the eucharistic meal reminds us to nurture one another through our daily meal habits: 'practising the Eucharist . . . is not only concerned with reason, faith and doctrine, but is also the bringing together of complex ingredients such as the body and senses, materiality and the Spirit, culture and the construction of meaning'.[15]

The mysticism found in sharing around a meal table is hard to describe, easy to miss, and Méndez-Montoya acknowledges this when describing eating a meal he had prepared for friends: 'I would say of what happened during our meal that "nothing definite can here be stated" [but] the sense of mystery unfolding . . . this experience of eating was "religious" or "divine" . . . an experience of the sacred'.[16] He concludes that eating enhances awareness of the body, 'allowing corporeal and material experience to become a primary source of reflection'.[17]

It is a very hard process to use words to explain and describe what we have seen and learned through a communal Eucharist, to share the awe and wonder of the opening and revealing of God through this ritual which we initially regarded as a mere practice of faithful memory. Our experience and encounter with the Divine has expanded and can only be understood within the realms of mystery:

> Christian mysticism is grounded in the revelation of Jesus Christ . . . [and] include[s] Christ revealed in the incarnation, in the Eucharist, in Scripture, and in the community of faith . . . [and] in the transformation of God's people. This transformation always results in missional action in the world.[18]

Conclusion

The grace of God has drawn us together as a community, and via the unexpected grace and welcome offered to us by the Church of England, we have entered into that grace more fully as we have wrestled with the practice and meaning of the Eucharist. This is for us the true blessing of a sacrament.

Notes

1 J. D. G. Dunn, *Jesus Remembered: Christianity in the Making*, Eerdmans, Grand Rapids, 2003, p. 481.

2 Nancy Eiesland, cited in Thomas E. Reynolds, *Vulnerable Communion: A Theology of Disability and Hospitality*, Brazos Press, Grand Rapids, 2008, p. 207.

3 Thomas E. Reynolds, *Vulnerable Communion: A Theology of Disability and Hospitality*, Brazos Press, Grand Rapids, 2008, p. 31.

4 Reynolds, *Vulnerable Communion*, p. 32.

5 Jean Vanier, *The Broken Body*, Anglican Book Centre, Toronto, 1988, p. 81.

6 Vanier, *Broken Body*, pp. 82–3.

7 Vanier, *Broken Body*, p. 83.

8 Elisabeth Moltmann-Wendel, *A Land Flowing with Milk and Honey*, SCM Press, London, 1986, p. 50.

9 Moltmann-Wendel, *Land Flowing with Milk and Honey*, p. 65.

10 Moltmann-Wendel, *Land Flowing with Milk and Honey*, p. 65.

11 Archbishop of Canterbury's Commission on Urban Priority Areas, *Faith in the City: A Call for Action by Church and Nation*, Church House Publishing, London, 1985.

12 *Faith in the City*, pp. 62–3.

13 Angel F. Méndez Montoya, *Theology of Food: Eating and the Eucharist*, Wiley-Blackwell, Chichester, 2012, p. 5.

14 Méndez Montoya, *Theology of Food*, pp. 8–9.

15 Méndez Montoya, *Theology of Food*, p. 12.

16 Méndez Montoya, *Theology of Food*, p. 16.

17 Méndez Montoya, *Theology of Food*, p. 29.

18 E. A. Heath, *The Mystic Way of Evangelism: A Contemplative Vision for Christian Outreach*, Baker Academic, Grand Rapids, 2008, p. 15.

12

The Transcendent Journey: Developing a Pilgrimage Model of the Eucharist

SUE WALLACE

There is a quote from the film *Field of Dreams* (Universal, 1989) that has stuck in my mind for many years: 'You know, we just don't recognize the most significant moments of our lives while they're happening.' It is often small coincidences or supposedly insignificant invitations that ultimately lead to big differences in the way we lead our lives, and such a moment happened with my first experience of planning a worship event in a cathedral space. I first had the opportunity to set up worship in the gloriously transcendent space of York Minster in the 1990s as part of diocesan youth events, and there is something wonderful about using a cathedral space by night in particular. The space itself, the lighting, the atmosphere and the wonder speak of the majesty of God in a way that many sermons would find hard to replicate. There is an atmosphere of romance attached to a cathedral space, and a sense, even to atheists, that a cathedral has had an extraordinarily long journey.

Years later when I became a voluntary chaplain in York Minster I noticed that the visitors would be filled with wonder. They puzzled over the fact that such an enormous space could have been built without the aid of power tools in an age in which the surrounding population were living in wattle and daub huts. The concept of time in a cathedral can feel completely different from that in most other contexts. Cathedrals demonstrate what Brian Eno would refer to as 'The Long

Now', and this resonates with many spiritual seekers, and also with those who do not even know that they are seeking. Even a twenty-first-century traveller can feel very small when placed in a building that soars above them and that they know will be standing when they have long since returned to dust and ashes. Later, when I came to plan multimedia worship services in that same space of York Minster, I was acutely aware that whatever we planned, we needed to allow space for that building to speak for itself and communicate that sense of transcendence to others.

Having come from a background in alternative worship, one of the things that struck me about cathedral worship was that most services, even midweek services, had an 'audience' as well as a congregation. The congregation itself is a gathered and unique one, containing visitors from many different countries of the world, and a number of different traditions. Yet there are others who lurk in the shadows or who hover in the distance, often hiding behind a barrier or a pillar. These people are the audience, and I would argue that this audience is deeply significant and important. I have always been fascinated by these other visitors; those who sometimes leap out from behind a pillar and take a photograph at a significant liturgical moment such as the elevation of the bread during the Great Thanksgiving of the eucharistic prayer or the moment of blessing at the end of the service. I often ponder what it is that makes them leap at such moments in the liturgy? Do they sense that something important is happening or do these gestures simply make a 'good photograph' for reasons of balance or symmetry?

One of the things which attracted me to cathedral worship, and ultimately led me towards cathedral ministry, was the fact that cathedrals themselves feel like a fresh expression of church. This is a statement which may sound ironic because of the extremely solid nature of cathedrals; they are almost the epitome of the 'inherited model' of church. And even in the most atheistic of circles there is often a strong sense of a cathedral city owning and loving their own cathedral building, even among those city-dwellers who would never go within the doors of the church to worship. There are many points of contact between the Christian community and the wider world in cathedral life which mirror the 'service to the community' aspect of a fresh expression, and cathedrals are often a source of social capital which do not require any kind of belief in God. Most cathedrals can be taken at many different levels. In one secular sense they function as a kind of museum, art gallery or school; there is much beauty to discover and many interesting historical tales to explore within these ancient spaces. For those who wish to go further in their journey of belonging there is a bank of volunteers to join, offering companionship to the lonely, and a chance to develop a wide range of gifts and talents including historical guiding, concert stewarding, embroidery, work with flowers, singing or bellringing to name but a few.

Other soft points of entry into the worshipping community include the music of the cathedrals, which is of a professional standard. Choral Evensong, which occurs daily in many historical cathedrals, is a service with a high musical content, which does not make great demands of the congregation and which attracts lovers of classical music who may not have any faith of their own. Even ardent atheist Richard Dawkins is quoted in the *Spectator* as having a 'Certain love for Choral Evensong'. Alongside this is an opportunity for children to grow and learn musical skills while singing in the cathedral choir or participating in the choral outreach opportunities, and a number of regular members of our cathedral community in Winchester initially started out as choir parents, being drawn into the church through its musical life.

Yet there is another entry point to cathedral life, that of the pilgrim. Pilgrimage has become increasingly important to spiritual seekers and more people than ever are walking the ancient pilgrimage routes such as the Camino of St Iago de Compostela or the Canterbury Way. In the summer months almost every week I give a blessing to a group who are travelling on this particular kind of spiritual journey, and some of these groups are very large. However, not all pilgrims make a lengthy journey; some simply come to light a candle, visit the remains of the tomb of St Swithun or write a tentative prayer on a piece of paper and place it on the prayer-board. In York Minster these numbers of prayerful pilgrims are very large indeed, judging by the 15,000 votive candles that the head verger used to order every month when I was in York. The only thing these candles were used for was visitors' prayers.

In 2006 the emerging church community I was part of, Visions in York, moved into the crypt of York Minster for six months when our own church building was being repaired. While we were there we encountered some of these pilgrims who came to our service, and yet we could see that our very informal style of Eucharist was not reaching those who tentatively came to spectate during this service and hide in the shadows. I have written about this journey in my chapter in *Ancient Faith, Future Mission: Fresh Expressions in the Sacramental Tradition* but one thing we discovered that is important to this conversation is the fact that those spiritual seekers we encountered were seeking a transcendent experience, but one which was also approachable.

The Eucharist itself is a great mystery, and one in which something deeply significant is happening, whatever our theological position of what happens to the bread and wine. Over time we found that being too informal within such a historic space, working against its atmosphere of awe, simply didn't work, and scared off those very people we were trying to reach, who wanted to hide in the shadows rather than being drawn into a close and informal circle. Yet these self-same spiritual travellers seemed also to be put off by too formal a welcome, bright lighting and a rigid rules of congregation engagement in the liturgy. They seemed to enjoy contemplation of the sacred, but also seemed to enjoy relaxing on a beanbag by candlelight, having permission to watch or to explore the building in prayer.

I would suggest that it is easy to make one of two mistakes. Either we dumb down the transcendence and disguise the enormous significance of what is happening as we meet Christ around his table, or we become mysterious in an off-putting way by being too obscure and unwelcoming, fencing off the holy table from visitors by not allowing those who have no knowledge of church or even the story of Christ to be easily drawn further into the sacramental life of the church community.

In the light of this tension I suggest two possible approaches to a Pilgrimage model of the Eucharist, which allow seekers to be draw into the sacramental journey that is taking place. The first of these approaches is one which actually uses the entire space of the available building. When we first started doing the Transcendence services in York they booked the entire cathedral for us. Initially we began in the cathedral crypt but soon realized that the crypt was too cramped with attendees to be able to have any kind of procession, and we particularly wanted to have a procession with the gospel book. Because of this we realized that if we wanted to take the gospel on a journey we would have to go with it and so we accidentally discovered just how powerful that gospel-journey itself was in a cathedral by night. We sang simple chants as we carried the gospel book to a corner of the cathedral which resonated with the theme of the service. The most memorable of these journeys was during a service about the wise and foolish builders when we took the gospel underground into the museum based in a cavern underneath the central tower where photographs of huge cracks in the stonework showed the damage uncertain foundations had caused, while we looked around at the giant concrete shoes which were constructed to enclose and save the pillars of the tower. In other Transcendence services we visited the crib, the font or a war memorial constructed to choristers who died in the First World War, and each time the outward pilgrimage around the building seemed to mirror the journeys that people were making in their hearts.

Another aspect of this, which became even more important for us, was the journey of prayer that also took place in these services. We always had a section of the service when we would simply let the congregation loose within the building, and they could encounter and use prayer stations or go on their own personal pilgrimage around the space while music played or a quartet sang. Later a bell rang, and we were encouraged to come and gather around the Holy Table, which was sometimes in a completely different part of the building from the opening worship.

When I moved to Leeds Parish Church I remembered how powerful those journeys were, and in some ways tried to replicate them, for example in a crib service that visited various grouped characters from the nativity story, poised to go on their journey in different corners of the church, or in our baptism services where we began in a place of the word and travelled to the font at the back of the church, informally gathering around it to actually baptize. When Leeds Parish Church became a Minster this idea of pilgrimage was taken up within the Minster-Making service itself, as different parts of the building (such as the altar, the font, and the church doors) echoed our four Minster values of prayer, mission, service and hospitality to the city. Even within the informal café-church Eucharist which took place in our church school, we found that moving to a completely different room for the eucharistic prayer of thanksgiving created a very special atmosphere, as children gathered around a decorated table which became a kind of grotto, with twinkling lights and draped fabrics of velvet, voile and gauze. Entering the eucharistic space through a doorway mirrored the thresholds that we crossed internally as we came to take our place around the table and seekers were swept along on that journey too, while also having several opportunities to place themselves where they wished to be in relation to the liturgical action.

The second approach to a Pilgrimage model of the Eucharist relies less on the physical space and more on the opportunities to go on an internal journey. Within our cathedral school we have been looking at ways to draw our children more fully into the eucharistic community, and this made me ponder the similarities with those spiritual seekers who are also in need of knowledge about the liturgy but who would probably not respond well to a lecture about the significance of Communion. With our cathedral schoolboys we did this by having a teaching Eucharist (not in itself a new thing) where we explained the various parts of the liturgy as we worshipped, but we did not necessarily do this with the spoken word. Easy access to data projection has given us great opportunities to bring in visual teaching too. One slide that I used at the beginning of the eucharistic prayer of thanks over the bread and wine, showed a picture of the Tardis and the words 'Communion is like a time machine, taking us to the foot of the cross'. These words were never spoken, they were simply there to be read if people wanted to do so. The boys love *Doctor Who*, and finding cultural touching points to draw others onward on their internal pilgrimage is important. In some ways the words of the liturgy were stripped down, and every opportunity to use 'other suitable words' was taken and the words were chosen carefully to culturally connect. It is also important to draw in those who have a more visual or kinaesthetic learning style upon the journey, which is why we also used symbols, action and song. There are a number of simple chants that can help draw the congregation into the action without them even realizing that they are also being taught. One example of this is 'Listen now for the gospel alleluia, it is God's word that changes us. Alleluia'. It can be sung with drum accompaniment, which also helps draw in those who are more activist. Symbols and actions can help the service become more experiential and so we passed a globe around during the prayers, and asked the boys to say the name of a country upon it. We all responded with the traditional response 'Lord in your mercy hear our prayer', and we then, very literally, offered our world to God by placing the globe itself upon the table. Another active moment which drew them into the Great Thanksgiving prayer was at the offering, when, rather than collecting money, we collected things that the children were thankful for. I was quite moved by the basic nature of the things they offered. 'Clean water, a bed, our school, enough food to eat'. I then wove some of these into a very short eucharistic preface 'and now we give you thanks for . . .' Once again there was space for awe and wonder and activity. If I could also have offered a literal journey by having different parts of the service in different rooms, I would have done so, but the building we were using wasn't suitable for this. However, it was clear by the time we reached the eucharistic prayer that they were far more engaged in the worship than in previous school services, and perhaps the most telling evidence for this was the boy who offered 'this service' as his suggestion for something to be thankful for.

Looking back at the eucharistic pilgrimages I have taken, in York Minster, in Leeds, in café church and in school buildings, I can say that there are always opportunities to add a pilgrimage element to any eucharistic celebration and by doing so we have an opportunity to draw in the 'audience' on the fringes of our worship. They are then no longer spectators but fellow travellers on a spiritual journey leading somewhere wonderful, and we never quite know where that might lead us too.

PART 5

Sacraments of Healing, Confession and Reconciliation

Are any among you sick? They should call for the elders of the church and have them pray over them, anointing them with oil in the name of the Lord. The prayer of faith will save the sick, and the Lord will raise them up; and anyone who has committed sins will be forgiven. (James 5.14–15)

If we confess our sins, he who is faithful and just will forgive us our sins and cleanse us from all unrighteousness. (1 John 1.9)

All this is from God, who reconciled us to himself through Christ, and has given us the ministry of reconciliation; that is, in Christ God was reconciling the world to himself, not counting their trespasses against them, and entrusting the message of reconciliation to us. So we are ambassadors for Christ, since God is making his appeal through us; we entreat you on behalf of Christ, be reconciled to God. (2 Corinthians 5.18–20)

Introduction

In many ways these sacraments/sacramentals are the hardest to write about because they relate to situations when things have or are going wrong for the fresh expression or for individuals in the mission initiative. Adrian Chatfield's Chapter 13 is a crucial scene-setter to understand the place of healing, grace and forgiveness as essential sacraments/sacramentals vital for any expression of church to become sustainable.

Bryony Davis's Chapter 14 guides us on how to approach supporting people when they come face to face with bad life decisions or situations of deep regret and shame, where it is extremely important they are handled well. Her reflections on confession then are helpful in how we approach this when people have to face themselves and what they have done

Julie Leger Dunstan's Chapter 15 shows just how important it is to have spiritual directors involved in mission initiatives, and offers great wisdom on how to support people to find faith even in very difficult personal circumstances.

Simon Sutcliffe's Chapter 16 shows great wisdom concerning reconciliation when a mission initiative goes wrong or does not work out, which requires a careful process of listening and relational reconciliation.

13

'What I have I give you': The Healing Sacraments

ADRIAN CHATFIELD

All life is sacramental: God wills it so, and it could not be otherwise. For those who have eyes to see and ears to hear, a falling leaf or a chance conversation may be both that and the quiet but insistent presence of a God who inhabits the world in all its fractured beauty.

When I prepared for confirmation at the age of nine, part of my reading was an old illustrated Anglo-Catholic catechism of my father's. I have a vivid memory of one picture, of a church with rain falling on it. There were seven drainpipes coming down from the roof; the rain was entitled GRACE, and each of the drainpipes carried the name of a sacrament. I loved the sense of the heavy rain of God's grace falling without measure, and I value the idea that grace is channelled through the sacramental life of the church. Where I took exception with the image even as a child was the idea that grace can somehow be contained or confined by the institution.

The twin themes of *abundant* grace, given and revealed in countless individual acts and events, and *channelled* grace, given through the Church's formal and structured liturgies, form the focus of this chapter. The routines of the Church's sacramental life guarantee that God's grace is given, but do not define the limits of that self-giving.

Grace is given, both formally and informally, so that the time will come when there is 'no more mourning and crying and pain', a time of *shalom*, made possible by Christ's gift of salvation and fulfilled by the work of the Holy Spirit. Towards that end, the pastoral work of the Church in healing, guiding, sustaining and reconciling is carried out in significant measure by the outpouring of Christ's grace in the sacraments and sacramental acts of the Church. We will here deal with three such acts: the sacraments of healing and reconciliation, and the ministry of deliverance: each contributes to the *shalom* of the individual, of the Church and of the kingdom of God among us.

Healing

'Healing on the streets', pioneered in 2005 by Mark Marx of the Causeway Coast Vineyard Church in Coleraine, Northern Ireland, is a classic illustration of the missional DNA of a sacramental ministry. A Church of Scotland-sponsored website says of this movement that it 'enables you to connect with your community every week, powerfully expressing God's love outside of the church walls. Over time you may find you build relationships, create stepping stones for people to come to Jesus, and see them healed along the way.'[1]

This contains several hints for a theologically grounded praxis. First is the fact that the sacraments are not limited to a holy domain, as all space is or may be sacred. Increasingly, in new missional contexts, the 'sanctuary' is formed by the presence of God's people going out, reaching outwards. Holiness is centrifugal.

Second, sacramental ministry, especially in a healing context, is not exclusively for those who are disciples of Christ. Recent Anglican liturgical thought on the sacrament of initiation has recognized that people are 'on the way' on a journey of faith, and may avail themselves of the formal sacrament at different points on the journey.[2] Similarly, the healing ministry is offered to all out of the generosity of God's grace, and people respond as they are able. The offering of prayer is unconditional, the outcome is gifted by God, and though we long for a formal response from the individual, that is not in the first instance why we offer it.

Third, as we all know, the outcome of a healing ministry is complex. Many of us have been disappointed that no one in our gatherings actually got up out of the wheelchair, though we all know stories of those who have. A relocating of the ministry of healing into the public square helps us to recover the intent of all the sacraments: the building of a kingdom community where we are recovering wholeness together by being re-formed as the people of God. When one is prayed for, all are touched by God.

This raises for some the question about who is authorized to minister the sacrament of healing, which leads to a fourth point. Just as the grace of God is channelled into the church normatively through those ritual acts we denominate as sacraments, so specific ministers are authorized. This is regular ecclesial practice, variously justified in a range of denominations. But just as the grace of God may not be captured or contained or limited by the institution, so the exercise of this ministry by others in exceptional or missional contexts may not be excluded as a possibility. This is not mere pragmatism: new sacraments may emerge, new ministers may be identified. By grace, we are called to experiment, that all may be touched by that grace. There is no need to be defensive about, or protective of, the grace of God.[3]

Finally, those who receive this sacramental touch are valued by God and his Church, and so learn that they too are called to participate in the kingdom work of the sacraments. To be healed is to be equipped, and perhaps it is here most appropriately that we recognize our call to be wounded healers.

The last part of this all too brief comment on the sacrament of healing needs to address the way it is carried out in new and unchurched contexts. Bearing in mind that we are not just dealing with the 'pastoral care of the sick' but equally with the 'missional reach of the church to the excluded', there are some simple guidelines:

- This is a ministry of inclusion into a community, and should look like a community action. In James, the 'elders' in chapter 5 are plural, and the current practice of having a singular sacramental minister does not look much like New Testament practice.

- Note that in the same letter, the elders are invited to pray 'over' rather than 'for' the sick person. Touch, as one of the senses, is a spiritually and theologically significant aspect of sacramentality. The physical closeness signifies the presence of God, the invitation to community and the gift of love.[4]
- Oil, lots of it, and oil that smells good, is of the essence of this sacrament both in its biblical antecedents and in current cultural context. There is a drabness about the way in which so many sacraments are performed perfunctorily in today's church, and we compete in an increasingly sensory market. Healing is a gift that God wants to lavish on his people as he restores them to himself and to each other, and unstinting love is signed with overflowing oil, 'precious oil on the head, running down upon the beard'.[5]

Reconciliation

Forty years ago, I heard the confession of a single mother who was prostituting herself in order to put her young daughter through school. This three-way conversation between her, her priest and her God enabled priestly advice to be given, which led to her building a shack on common land and the claiming of her squatter's rights.[6] Some 20 years later, at an open-air act of worship, I asked another woman to give her testimony of recent conversion. She chose to speak to the gathered assembly and curious passers-by of adultery, marital breakdown, repentance, forgiveness and the transformative power of the grace of God. Both stories, one from a formal ecclesial setting and the other more informal, charismatic and contemporary, bear witness to the *shalom* that comes when sin is dealt with radically and sacramentally.

At the end of the *Canterbury Tales*, Geoffrey Chaucer has his Parson deliver a sombre assessment of the human state and the need for repentance. The three steps in his exposition of the sacrament are contrition, confession and satisfaction, and we will use these three steps to comment on the missional impact of the sacrament of reconciliation in the life of new expressions of church.

Gitta Sereny, in her study of the extermination camp commandant Rudolf Hoess,[7] wrote about the way in which he would speak to her easily of his work in the camp, or of his exemplary family life, but never of both in the same conversation. The day came when one conversation 'leaked' accidentally into the other, and shortly thereafter he died of a heart attack. His case is illustrative of how hard we find it to be honest with ourselves about ourselves. The burden is just too great. Contrition is the first great consequence of coming to terms with ourselves, the first step towards freedom, a breaking of the lie that we tell ourselves, that we are really all right just as we are. The Church is today called to proclaim the counter-cultural word that truth-telling leads to sorrow and opens the door for grace.

Almost as hard is voicing the truth that one has discovered. This for me is the most powerful human aspect of the sacrament: of course we do not need to tell another. It is in a proper sense a matter entirely between me and God, as evangelicals are quick to remind us. However, it signals two key elements: first, that there exists a community of grace which does not hold us hostage to our past or define us by it. And second, that the work of holiness is not a work which I undertake while you stand in the wings watching and checking. Holiness is a shared enterprise, with the Holy Spirit, and with the community of reconciliation.

The third and final component in Chaucer's Parson's list is satisfaction, an action undertaken not to achieve forgiveness, but as a discipline and as an act, where possible, of restorative justice. It is all very well and good to say that forgiveness is the free act of God. True repentance demands justice done, restoration begun, and active engagement with the consequences of one's former actions. There is an appropriate repayment, a rebuilding of a kingdom damaged by what we have done. I have on occasion 'imposed' a penance that echoed the character of the wrong committed, in the belief that it might engender a sense both of responsibility and of reparation.[8]

The last element of the sacramental act is the declaration of forgiveness, coupled with the priestly absolution. There is no space here to expand on the theology of absolution. Suffice it to say that the power of the Word spoken over the sinner who repents focuses not on the one who speaks it, but on the fact that it is spoken by another, by one who in the Christian community has the authority and responsibility in this case to proclaim that God forgives all those who truly repent. Certainly when I made my own confession at the age of nine – to my parish priest who happened to be my father – I felt an enormous sense of relief, of a weight gone, an action absolutely completed, not by him, but by God.

Deliverance

The Church in England has with notable exceptions lost its sacramental vision of a struggle fought 'against the cosmic powers of this present darkness' using the whole arsenal of weapons made available to us by the grace, authority and power of a victorious God. Christ's atonement for us is not simply a passport to a future better life. It is, as every African Christian knows, the power under which life may be made more wholesome today. Enlightenment scepticism, coupled with a fear of abusive practices and the proper need for safeguarding, mean that many Western Christians have consigned the language of 'exorcism' to a genre of horror movies, Dennis Wheatley novels and eccentric sects.

The Chinese church is not so coy. One of the classics of that persecuted flourishing community is Watchman Nee's *Sit, Walk, Stand*, a popular exposition of Paul's Epistle to the Ephesians. In the last section, on chapter 6, Nee says of our spiritual warfare that 'God has committed himself to his servants to act through them as they take action "in the name" . . . All that takes place results from the impact of the name of the Lord Jesus on the situation, and *they are authorized to use that name*.'[9]

Bearing in mind the appropriate cautions, warnings and codes of conduct that it is right for us to observe, let me highlight three sacramental actions which are an integral part of this ministry, which the Church is called to exercise authoritatively, with joy and in Christ's power. They are the related actions of blessing, of cleansing, and of protecting.

> The business of blessing is . . . not only a matter of acknowledging that things come from God but also a recognition that everything that comes under the shadow of God's grace . . . is being drawn to God as the one in whom it will find its eternal fulfilment.[10]

We go on the offensive for the kingdom first of all proactively by signing, sealing and consecrating, by 'writing God' all over the world. It is as if the sacramental act of blessing were a kind of divine graffiti, not defacing the creation nor effacing human effort, but restoring the proper creative identity of things.

That is why, much as I am aware of the magical presuppositions that often attach themselves to the act of blessing,[11] I have always delighted in being asked to come and declare the name of God and the goodwill of a playful Creator over cars, houses, boats, blast furnaces and a multitude of other bits and pieces during a long and fun-filled ministry. To bless that which we own and occupy is to declare that it is both God's and ours, to be used and enjoyed in dialogue rather than in possessive isolation. It is also, of course, to assert that the evil one possesses nothing, owns nothing, and is a usurping fraud.

Where we recognize that some such usurpation has taken place, the Church's vocation is to cleanse. Not to explain, but to cleanse. It is remarkable how much time academically overtrained ministers spend in trying to make sense of the universe to our parishioners, when the almost universal cry is not 'Explain!' but 'Help!' As one who rarely understands what exactly is going on when I pray around a troubled house, I take the pragmatic line that God understands, prayer works, and people are relieved. It would be injudicious of us to advertise a cleansing ministry too publicly, because we would be besieged by cranks, voyeurs and mischief-makers. We need nonetheless to find a way of making the cleansing ministry of the Church more visible and less secretive. The best way of doing this would be to encourage the practice of bringing stuff to church. We do this at harvest, but rarely at any other time of year. The stuff of life should be brought for blessing, and the stuff of life damaged, stinted or blocked should be brought for cleansing. Perhaps the somewhat odd story of the handkerchiefs in Acts 19 serves as a model: the handkerchief is a sacramental token to be taken to the sick. Might not a reverse version of this be the bringing of a token of the thing or place needing cleansing into the company of God's people?

The third sacramental act – that of protecting – takes us back to the starting point of this chapter. All life is sacramental: it is our task not just to proclaim that, but to help people envision a world in which more is happening than simply meets the eye. God is always present, and though he is often 'behind the scenes', his presence and his intervening activity both console and enable life to continue. I knew a training minister once, who sat in on his curates' first funerals and weddings, behind the organ. It was remarkable how helpful they found that invisible reassurance! The sacramentals of protection are manifold: holding crosses, rosaries, medallions, pictures over the front door. We need to reintroduce what one historian of art has called visual piety,[12] and what we might call tangible piety: the tokens of the presence of God by which people in distress can know that God has not abandoned them.

Conclusion

To write about sacraments is in the end to write about a God 'with skin on', made flesh in Jesus Christ. We might say that Christ is the great sacrament, and that all our sacramental acts are performed as if Christ himself were doing them. That is what the doctrine of the real presence of Christ in the Holy Eucharist really means. It means too that the Church, as the body of Christ here on earth continuing to do 'these works, and greater than these', acts *in loco Christi* through the sacraments.

When we act, heaven breaks in, the kingdom comes a little closer, and the promise of *shalom* becomes real in one more person's life.

Notes

1 www.evangelismideas.org/idea.aspx?id=459 – accessed 30.8.2016.

2 Michael Perham, *On the Way: Towards an Integrated Approach to Christian Initiation*, Church House Publishing, London, 1995.

3 Andrew Davison helpfully says in his book *Blessing* that blessing 'is a priestly action, which is not to say that it is an activity restricted to those who have received the office of priest or bishop through ordination', Canterbury Press, Norwich, Kindle locations 2508–9.

4 Lizette Larson-Miller, *Lex Orandi: The Sacrament of Anointing the Sick*, Liturgical Press, Collegeville, 2005, p. 12.

5 Psalm 133.2.

6 For those who are rightly concerned about the seal of the confessional, this story has been heavily altered and disguised.

7 Gitta Sereny, *Into That Darkness: From Mercy Killing to Mass Murder*, Picador Books, London, 1977.

8 Mennonite writing on the subject is worth exploring further. See for example https://peacetheology.net/pacifism/biblical-bases-for-restorative-justice/ and the links with Paul's ministry of reconciliation in 2 Corinthians 5.

9 Author's emphasis. Watchman Nee, 1977, *Sit, Walk, Stand*, Tyndale House Publishers, Wheaton, 1977, p. 62.

10 Davison, *Blessing*, Kindle edition location 1295–7.

11 Well documented historically in Keith Thomas, *Religion and the Decline of Magic*, Penguin, London, 2003.

12 David Morgan, *Visual Piety: A History and Theory of Popular Religious Images*, University of California Press, Berkeley, 1998.

14

The Sacrament of Confessions and Reconciliation: Reflections Growing Out of a Prison Chaplaincy Context

BRYONY DAVIS

Culturally, sin is a tricky issue. In a society where there are few accepted absolutes, people measure their behaviour against their own internal truths, judge their actions as to 'what is right for me' and are suspicious of external moral authorities. In addition, many of the words of our faith vocabulary which describe our understanding of sin and forgiveness are no longer in common usage. This may partly explain why confession has become one of the most marginal of the sacraments, little practised across much of the Church. A church which struggles to express the concept of sin in ways that connect to people beyond its walls, often ends up sounding outdated, narrow-minded and judgemental. Where it is difficult to speak of sin, it is harder still to promote the practice of confession. Yet society exhibits many signs of disease. Addiction is prevalent – not just to drugs or alcohol, but to gambling, pornography and unhealthy relationships with food, overwork, ambition and exercise. Problems with mental health are growing and people are more anxious and stressed than ever before, concealing deep-seated shame about the way they look, their abilities or achievements. Yet in this sense of brokenness, shame and failure lies an opportunity to connect with people spiritually and to bring the gospel's gifts of forgiveness and release, if we can find new ways to offer and express this sacrament.

Prison chaplaincy is an interesting place from which to explore these themes. By their nature, prisons are places where individuals are brought face to face with their wrongdoing and where many of the distractions and amusements that we use to divert ourselves from the more difficult side of human nature are stripped away. In prison, it is harder to hide. The mistakes and failings which have taken away your freedom are laid bare. In my experience, it is often a refreshingly real place. People are more honest about who they are and the mess they are in and there is an openness to spiritual exploration from those with little previous experience of faith. This lies in contrast to many parish settings, where weakness and failure are often kept well hidden and people (both inside and outside the church) rarely speak of or perhaps even perceive their need for God.

My own context, as an Anglican chaplain in a large, busy women's prison, brought me into contact with a large number of people who were completely unchurched, alongside those with some degree of faith or church experience. While prison chaplaincy is neither a traditional model nor fresh expression of church, it brings together elements of both, and is a fruitful place to gain insights that might inform practice within fresh expressions, perhaps especially those working in more deprived communities. Prison populations are of course marked by a high degree of dysfunction and trauma. Many prisoners have significant mental health problems, poor physical health, the experience of childhood abuse or domestic violence, struggles with addictions and poor levels of social support or integration. This is compounded by poor levels of literacy and educational attainment, unemployment and homelessness, and for many the repeated experience of returning to prison again and again. Carrying life stories filled with pain, exclusion and failure, it is unsurprising that those in prison have a keen sense and understanding of human brokenness and sinfulness.

In parallel runs my participation in holy::ground, a small missional community based in affluent, urban Surrey, with its roots in the Anglican and Methodist Church. This group gathers those who struggle with church for a range of reasons, and places a high importance on building community, encouraging honest relationships, on creativity, contemplation, experimentation and participation in worship and faith exploration. This provides a useful counterbalance to the world of prison and a different perspective from which to view this sacrament.

It is worth noting that the practice of the sacrament of confession has changed significantly throughout church history, waxing and waning it its observance and form. Biblical texts encourage the practice of mutual confession (James 5.16) and make connections to the maintenance of church order (Matthew 18.15–18); with public acts of confession emerging in the first few centuries as the solution to post-baptismal sin. Initially, this was offered as a 'once only' opportunity to atone for the most serious post-baptismal sin, rather than as a regular and routine matter.[1] Later, individual confession grew into a more regular practice, in addition to communal confession becoming enshrined within church liturgy. Medieval times saw an approach that was both punitive and commercial, bringing the sacrament into disrepute. Post-reformation, the Western church turned against individual priest-led confession, leaving only its liturgical form. Revived by the Oxford Movement, current practice varies widely, with individual confession maintained within more catholic traditions and communal confession widely used within liturgical churches. Less traditional models of church have often confined confession to their repertoire of songs, losing the individual and liturgical aspects altogether. These historic forms, of mutual, individual and corporate confession, are useful to take into our thinking on the use of confession within fresh expressions.

That the sacrament of confession comes with such a varied history has advantages. The liturgical constraints, which confine Holy Communion and Baptism, within some denominations, do not apply; and its practice is less contentious. It is also a sacrament that is not associated with specific physical symbolism – no prescribed sign of water, bread and wine, rings or oil. This gives the flexibility to be creative as to how the sacrament can be reimagined. There is a freedom to take the underlying gift and allow it to be born afresh in any number of different ways, while remaining rooted in the tradition of the Church.

When reflecting on my experience of the past few years, both working in prison and within a small missional community, the following areas seem important.

Humility – In a society that values strength, independence and success it can be hard for people to own weakness and failure. This image is strongly projected by the media and even our churches can seem full of people whose relationships are flourishing, families happy, children well-adjusted, jobs purposeful, leisure-time fulfilling and bank balances healthy. It can feel lonely to admit to depression or redundancy or to share the struggles of life, let alone to having messed up, hurt people or made mistakes. Leaders can do much to model humility that owns their own weakness and admits when they are wrong. My experience is that transparency is catching and when a few are brave enough to talk about life's difficulties in ways that are real, others will follow. Of course there need to be boundaries in sharing appropriately and safely in any situation, but creating a safe space where people can be real and own their imperfections is fundamental to helping them bring those imperfections to God.

Language – I have already mentioned that many of the ways we speak of sin and forgiveness are virtually confined to a religious context, or have quite negative overtones to those unfamiliar with church. If we want people from unchurched backgrounds to understand their need of forgiveness and for them to feel able to receive this gift from God, we need to talk in a language that connects. This might mean, in our teaching, prayers and liturgy, using more accessible terms to describe sin, rather than resorting to more religious terminology. For the women in prison, in both prayers of confession and teaching I would speak of 'the times we have hurt others', 'when we have let ourselves and others down', 'the things we are ashamed of', 'things we want to put right' and found that taking this gentler approach helped to reduce barriers. It helps disarms a tendency towards dualism, where sin only relates to 'bad people' and 'big stuff' like murder, mugging old ladies, offences against children and the like. We need to develop people's understanding that we all need forgiveness and all carry that innate human trait – the tendency to mess things up. Helping people to recognize that worry, pride, envy, overconsumption (both of food and belongings), and a whole range of other 'socially acceptable' sins is important. So too is accepting a share of the responsibility for society's sins; for example, our oppression of the weak through patterns of trade and employment; or our destruction of the environment through our wastefulness and overconsumption. Where the balance between individual and broader societal aspects of sin lies will very much depend on context.

Guilt and shame

There is an important counterbalance to helping people develop a broader sense of human sinfulness – the need to uphold a belief in the belovedness and essential goodness of humanity, as those created in God's image. The Christian church has often struggled to do this. This is crucial in our encounters with the many who carry a burden of shame. Here I am not referring to the specific sense of guilt for things they have done wrong, where a sense of remorse is appropriate for the harm done to another. Shame is the more pervasive feeling of unworthiness and failure, directed inward towards the self rather than focusing on the hurtful behaviour.[2] I have found it to be widespread among the women I have worked with in prison, many of whom have suffered abuse of one form or another or whose lives lack the experience of being loved, affirmed or valued. However, I believe it is common across all sections of society, although perhaps better hidden. Care needs to be taken not to drive already shame-laden people deeper into the cycle of self-depreciation. I have found it helpful to use times of liturgical confession to create space to bring the whole self – the things we are proud of as well as the things we are ashamed of; or gifts and strengths as well as our weakness and failings.

This holding the whole of who we are before God helps to avoid pushing people from appropriate guilt into unhelpful and destructive shame. Discerning between guilt and shame can be an important role of the confessor and is discussed later.

Opportunities for reflection

In a society addicted to entertainment and stimulation, it can be hard to encourage people to be still, even for a short while. I think it is quite hard, for those who grew up in more pedestrian times, where boredom was an accepted part of life, to understand the abject panic of many young adults today, when faced with silence or inactivity. Lives are lived in a constant stream of noise and communication; brains buzzing with music, visuals, messages and demands on their attention. Yet to enter into the experience of confession requires the ability to quieten ourselves for long enough to reflect on our how we are living and to face the lonely space inside. The prison setting at least has the advantage of compulsory time alone each day, with little in the way of occupation or distraction. This can create the beginnings of a more contemplative and thoughtful way of living. I have found teaching journaling, contemplative prayer, mindful colouring and the use of a simple, contemporary version of a daily examen helpful tools in encouraging people to be more comfortable in their own company, in slowing them down and allowing space to be open to God's spirit. Outside the prison environment, these are equally useful, but encouragement will be needed to create the time and space to practise them. At holy::ground, a regular midweek meal followed by a communal time of silence, used as individuals find most helpful, has contributed to providing some structure for those who find it difficult to set time aside alone.

Telling our stories

I have to admit that I have only heard formal sacramental confession on a few occasions within my prison ministry. Far more often, confessional moments have come as the result of giving people the opportunity to tell their story. Many of the women we work with have never been listened to or had anyone bear witness to their suffering and pain. There is something deeply humanizing about being heard, even though the stories shared often contain unbelievable trauma and suffering. As a chaplain, an important part of my role is attending carefully to these stories, affirming all that is good, the times they have shown courage, strength, love and perseverance; and drawing out the strands of brokenness, regret and guilt. Helping people to sift through the dark and damaged parts of their life, to discern what needs forgiveness and what needs letting go can be very healing. It can help to distinguish between guilt that needs dealing with and shame that is not theirs to bear, and gives a place to speak God's forgiveness. Within more mainstream ministry, I wonder how many opportunities people have for honest one-to-one conversation with a trusted 'other'? If, within fresh expressions of church, our only encounters are communal, fleeting or shallow, we will likely miss those confessional moments and the freedom they can bring.

Forgiveness as journey

If my time working with people in prison has taught me anything, it is that forgiveness is very often a complicated business! This is not always reflected as we rattle through a liturgical confession on a Sunday morning, with the implication that forgiveness can be arrived at in a single tidy act. Of course sometimes this is the case, but very often a process is needed – of recognizing our sin, accepting responsibility for our own actions, of ceasing to blame other people or our circumstances for our own failings. All this requires self-awareness and a willingness to be honest before God. More difficult still is being ready to receive the forgiveness God offers, to let go and move on to forgive ourselves. All this can take time, encouragement, and may need revisiting a number of times as awareness and acceptance deepens.

For some, forgiving self can be the hardest thing, especially when others have been harmed in ways that cannot be repaired. Again patience and repeated reassurance are often needed. For some, the verbal act of hearing words of absolution spoken directly to an individual by another (priest or otherwise) can be helpful. So can the use of more concrete activities to symbolize the receiving of forgiveness and a new beginning. Writing a letter of confession, which is then burnt during an act of absolution; or using water-based pens to write on white tiles and washing them clean in water can be powerful acts; as can anointing with oil; or sprinkling with water as a sign of the renewal of baptismal forgiveness.

In relation to forgiving others the path is no simpler. There is a real danger in pressurizing people to forgive those who have hurt them. This can lead to guilt where forgiveness feels impossible and can disrupt the necessary process of grieving for the harm done, which might well include stages of denial, anger, blame and despair. Where very significant harm has been suffered, it may be as much as a person can manage to bring their rage and inability to forgive before God, praying that in time they might find the will to forgive. Where there has been abuse or manipulation, care needs to be taken, so that untimely forgiveness will not open someone up to further mistreatment. A parishioner once said to me that they were only really able to forgive their controlling and emotionally abusive father, when they realized that they could do so without having to let him back into their life. Similarly, I have worried for victims of domestic violence, where unboundaried forgiveness could risk drawing them back into an abusive situation. Discerning the right time and being able to 'hold' someone as they journey through the forgiveness process is a significant gift and requires sensitivity and care.

The art of putting things right

The practice of penance does not have a very positive history, veering from harsh physical punishments and questionable financial obligations to a cursory recitation of a Hail Mary or two. Yet the act of making amends can be very healing, both for the wrongdoer and the person who was harmed. Within the criminal justice system, the practice of Restorative Justice has shown how powerful this can be. Victim and offender come together in a boundaried and supportive environment to explore the impact of the crime on all concerned and to look at what might be done to help repair the harm. These encounters are often profoundly healing for victims, who find a sense of release and strength to move on, and also can offer significant motivation for offenders to change. The model of confession and restoration also appears at the heart of Alcoholics Anonymous' 12-step programme, with the requirement to make a 'searching and fearless moral inventory; to admit the exact nature of our wrongs; and to make amends wherever possible to those we have harmed'. Again this process is seen as central to recovery and finding the strength to live differently.

This has challenged me to think about how, within the Church, we often miss the opportunity to help people to put things right. For individuals, learning to take practical action, in the form of an apology, an act of kindness, an attempt to change our behaviour or make amends can help to make repentance more meaningful. Where relationships are damaged and where leaders are skilled at helping people to listen to one another and move towards resolution, transformation is possible in a whole range of family, church, community and work conflicts. Likewise, encouraging taking action to take responsibility for our more corporate sins, perhaps campaigning for trade justice, switching to green energy, offsetting carbon emissions for example, could deepen and enrich our experience of confession.

Embedding confession

If we believe there are riches to be mined from the tradition of confession, we need to reflect on how, in each context, we can take these treasures into the lives of our fresh expressions. It is unlikely to take the form of a priest, sitting in a confession box each week, with a queue of penitents waiting their turn. A biblical model of mutual confession resonates when we create communities where people can be real and share honestly their weaknesses and failings. When it comes to drawing on the practice of liturgical confession, we might want to think about the spaces we create in our worship and prayer, in whatever form it takes, for self-reflection and openness before God. As well as carefully chosen words, we might want to enrich our acts of confession with images, music, movement and reflective activity, and there are lots of resources to help with this. It is important in this not to lose the power of absolution and to think how we speak God's words of forgiveness into confessional acts we create.

The liturgical year too can offer reminders of our need to take stock of our lives, with Advent, Ash Wednesday, Lent and Good Friday all nudging us towards repentance. Alternatively, the New Year lends itself to exploring how our lives might need to change. The Gospels too give a rich resource of stories, with diverse pictures of repentance and forgiveness – the prodigal son (Luke 15.11–22), the paralysed man (Luke 5.17–26), Zacchaeus (Luke 19.1–10), the woman caught in adultery (John 8.2–11), the thief on the cross (Luke 23.39–43), to name a few. These stories help us to break free from narrow and simplistic understandings of forgiveness and provide connections to our own experiences and the stories and struggles of our own church communities. When thinking how we might make room for individual opportunities for confession, leaders may need to be more intentional in giving time for people to meet with them one to one, and to develop confidence in talking with them about difficult things. This is not a skill everyone has, and leaders of fresh expressions need to identify those, lay or ordained, who might most appropriately exercise this area of ministry. Again, finding concrete and creative ways to help people engage with this process of owning and speaking of our failings, hearing and accepting God's forgiveness, forgiving ourselves and where possible making restoration can make confession accessible and meaningful. We might too wish to think about this sacrament more missionally, looking for 'confessional opportunities' within the wider community. Through our involvement in mediation, conflict resolution, restorative justice, or our support of 12-step programmes, we might find ways to take the riches of our Christian heritage beyond church walls.

Celebrating forgiveness

If there is one final thing to say, it is of the need to catch hold of the purpose of confession. The Roman Catholic Church was perceptive when it rebranded the sacrament of confession as the sacrament of reconciliation. It is easy to get caught up in the misery of human wrongdoing and the need for repentance, and to miss the point entirely – that confession is about being set free, proclaiming loudly that God is forgiveness and that a new start is possible. This is good news, wonderful news! In a world where so many people are crippled by guilt, feel inadequate or that they have failed, we have a unique gift to offer. If we let the sacrament of confession slip away into obscurity, we may deny people the joy and liberation of hearing the words: 'Your sins are forgiven'; of being able to lay down their burdens and walk tall, knowing they are, in the words of Helen Prejean, 'more than the worst thing they have ever done in their lives'.[3] This alone should motivate us to explore how the sacrament of confession might breathe forgiveness and reconciliation into our church communities, whatever form they take.

Notes

1 John Macquarrie, *Guide to the Sacraments*, SCM Press, Norwich, 2000, p. 93.

2 Dr Joseph Burgo, 'The difference between guilt and shame', www.psychologytoday.com/blog.

3 Helen Prejean (Roman Catholic nun and campaigner against the death penalty), *Dead Man Walking: An Eyewitness Account of the Death Penalty in the United States*, Random House, New York, 1993.

15

Absolve Means to Set Free: Confession, Mission and Spiritual Direction

JULIE LEGER DUNSTAN

The Desert Fathers told of how a high-ranking aristocrat from the city of Alexandria travelled to the hermitages of Scete to visit a renowned elder. Each day for three days the visitor attempted to engage the monk in talk about spirituality and theology, but although he received him hospitably, the elder spoke not a word in reply. Embarrassed on the visitor's behalf, the hermit's young disciple asked his master why he would not speak to the Alexandrian. 'He asks me about heavenly matters,' replied the master, 'and I know nothing of such things.' Suddenly understanding what the elder was teaching by his silence, the disciple advised the aristocrat to attempt a different approach. 'You must speak to him of the passions of your soul,' the visitor was told. Swallowing his pride, the aristocrat approached the elder with an open heart, sharing the struggles, failures and sins he had never allowed anyone else to know. At once, he received the words he had been seeking.[1]

I love this story because it illustrates rather well what I believe to be true: that we can only receive the words we most need, words of healing, forgiveness or wisdom, when our hearts are truly open. While we are unlikely to find a spiritual director who would refuse to talk to us in this way, we are all too likely to want to engage in safe talk about spirituality and theology and to seek the false consolations of so-called 'heavenly' matters. But to be truly 'pardoned, healed, restored, forgiven', we usually need soul-searching conversations with someone who invites and even challenges us to greater honesty. For this reason, spiritual direction could be considered a vitally important ministry in the arena of 'fresh expressions'; for both opening up the sacrament of confession as genuinely good news and modelling a more profound focus in mission and pastoral care.

There are many helpful definitions of spiritual direction. One that I like is from James Keegan, who writes:

> Spiritual direction is the contemplative practice of helping another person to awaken to the mystery called God in all of life, and to respond to that discovery in a growing relationship of freedom and commitment.[2]

Despite what the name suggests, this is not about someone directing another. It is about listening together to the direction of the Spirit in the life of the person seeking support in this way. Spiritual direction or accompaniment, as it is sometimes called, is *contemplative* because, perhaps like all true prayer, it is about creating the space to attend to the God who is both beyond and within. As well as contemplative it's also incarnational because it looks for that revelation of mystery in the mess and miracle of everyday life. I'll come back to the second half of this definition in a minute.

Of course spiritual direction is not, strictly speaking, a fresh expression of church; still, as it becomes more popular among individuals who may not be Christians or those who are estranged from the conventional Christian church, it could well be a 'fresh' and much needed communication of both mission and sacrament. In addition, a consideration of spiritual direction might also inform and resource those called to the missional edge between church and culture, including pioneers, missioners and evangelists. Specifically, increasing interest in the ministry of spiritual direction could point strongly to the need for a renewed sense of sacramental confession as part of pioneering or missional ministries and the need for creative and resonant expressions of this sacrament in the twenty-first century.

Spiritual direction as missional

To qualify, spiritual direction might have a missional quality if and as it returns to a more traditional understanding of itself, rooted in Scripture and the tradition and seeing itself as a ministry within the Church rather than simply a form of counselling. Rooted thus, the Christian spiritual director might at one glance be seen as that sort of minister described in the introduction to this book: one exercising the skill and art of 'triple listening', with an ear to God in prayer, the stories of those who come and the wisdom of the tradition.

While counselling might offer valuable support and even manifest the presence of God, as any encounter of love will, it does not give us the rich resources and wisdom of Scripture and theology. It does not often challenge us to look for the paradoxical or the prophetic. It does not invite us to follow Christ. On the other hand, spiritual direction is not mere theological reflection or Bible study in which we might find those resources and challenges but not always understand deeply how it could inform or transform our lives. And finally, spiritual direction is not just prayer in which we might earnestly seek guidance or healing but struggle to open fully and honestly without the presence of another to hear our failures and hopes and mediate the love of God to us.

Spiritual direction is the rich and fruitful overlap between an open-hearted encounter, an awareness of God, ever present in love, and the stories and insights of the Christian tradition. This is often especially appreciated by those who find themselves on the edge of the Church in some way, looking for authentic and personal ways to re-connect to God and to their faith. These conversations listen not just to the story being told but hold it alongside God's story in the presence of the Spirit. The fertile ground which lies between these realities is the very place where the seed of Christ can take root; or dormant disciples be nurtured to grow and blossom in maturity, wisdom and love.

Spiritual direction has always sat, necessarily, as an edge ministry. Perhaps one way it might locate itself among other ministries is by identifying itself not *as* but alongside other missional ministries; poised to communicate the love of God in a very profound way to those who come. It might also see itself as confessional in nature, not least because it offers the space inside which someone can reveal who they are – sin, sorrow and splendour – and be reconciled to themselves and to God. Spiritual direction offers both the world and the Church a sorely needed place for honest and transformative conversation about both who we are and who God is, in the midst of our ordinary lives; conversations that lead, as all true conversation does, to real conversion.

Spiritual direction as informing fresh approaches to the sacrament of confession

Traditionally, the sacrament of confession is an opportunity to reflect upon areas of 'sin', either privately in a liturgical setting or vocally in a one-to-one setting, and to receive absolution from an ordained priest. Despite its inherent value, it's easy to see at a glance the first obstacle for most people both in and, certainly, outside of the Church: the word sin has inherited a narrow and unhelpful meaning. It seems likely that the formal sacrament of confession is one of the more difficult to approach by those who call themselves 'spiritual but not religious' because it is often the very experience of harsh judgement and burdensome guilt that contributes to their alienation from the Church. It seems vital, then, that we find some fresh and authentic expression of all this for our time.

Spiritual direction, in the definition above from Keegan, helps another to discover the mystery of God in all of life – *and to respond to that discovery in a growing relationship of freedom and commitment.* I think freedom is a crucial word when trying to re-claim the place of 'confession' as creative and life-giving. Sin could be seen not so much as moral failure (even if it sometimes is) but more as a painful lack of freedom in relation to the greater vision and promises of God. To shape the experience of confession around the invitation to greater freedom rather than the primitive and punishing notions of sin that we carry around so stubbornly has been truly liberating to many people I have seen. Freedom to love and to be loved is at the heart of what all of us most deeply want and of what God most wants for us. To find that greater yes is to begin to find the courage to say no to all that blocks the love of Christ from growing in us. For those who sit outside the Church altogether, this yes to them may be what allows them to say their first tentative yes to God in return.

I recall many instances in my own spiritual direction work with others when simply reframing sin in this way yielded deep 'confession' – of failure and struggle and sin. The relief is palpable when someone crippled by guilt can feel that what they have brought can be held in love: neither minimized in the supremely secular light of self-fulfilment, nor demonized in a punishing Church, but instead put in the context of God's deep desire for them to become all that they were called to be – creative, beautiful, unique, whole. True judgement is always liberating. Confession then becomes a means of being set free and releases us to respond with greater commitment to the life of the Spirit.

That this sacred hour of sharing is sacramental is easy to argue. That the prayerful, compassionate and attentive listening of one to another is a visible sign of an invisible grace cannot, surely, be questioned. That this heartfelt encounter with God's love must inform any formal expression of sacramental confession is obvious. With all this agreed, and ideally in place, it must also be said that the authority of absolution as expressed by those in the ordained ministries provides an important additional grace: absolution delivered, if you will, from a visible representative of the Church can speak powerfully against the condemning authority figures from the past, residing inside the despair of so many.

Confession as good news for all

'He speaks of heavenly matters and I know nothing of such things.' Though we may on occasion be afforded glimpses of transcendent glory, we usually discover the mystery of God's love in the ordinary and vulnerable reality of our lives. The word we all most seek is not found in lofty ideals but in down-to-earth love and belonging. To be welcomed into that love and belonging is one way of understanding sacramental confession.

Jesus embodied this word of welcome again and again, but it could be heard and felt only by those who 'confessed' their need of it. Christ's mission was always to those who felt they didn't belong, to the oppressed and marginalized of society. And while spiritual direction is still not nearly accessible enough to those on the edge, I believe that insomuch as it reminds and allows those who do come to it to recognize and embrace the excluded and rejected parts within themselves, it brings them nearer to standing in solidarity with all those on the outside. Further, those within Christian communities who can express the deeper dimensions of confession in the way I have been describing can, by their much more open doors, welcome a greater diversity of people looking for that healing and reconciling love of God.

If it looks as though a one-to-one conversation in a safe room or church office is a million miles away from the refugee camps or the politically divided world – look again. To the extent that the stranger within ourselves and in our community is welcomed, the naked clothed, so I believe we come nearer to being able to see and embrace and clothe the stranger further afield. Insomuch as confession becomes a place where we divest and allow others to divest of power and persona, so it becomes subversive of destructive systems and becomes life-giving for those around us. Where inadequacy and sin can be known, felt about and expressed, confession becomes a place where the good news of the kingdom can be heard deeply. And when so heard, so communicated, with the power of authenticity and healing so needed in our world.

The first mark of mission is to proclaim the good news of the kingdom. The good news is that we are loved exactly as we are and not because we earn it or deserve it; not because we have perfectly articulated theology or successful lives. This distortion of God's love is ever present, even in those who 'know' better. How much more in those who don't – those who stand on the outside of the Church with little or no experience of the gospel or community. I often see a painful divide. On the one hand are people crying with need or cowering with shame, having little or no experience of God. On the other hand, people who can speak quite fluently of heavenly matters and the love of God but their hearts remain defended and circumscribed. The gift of true confession is immense: the place where honest conversation of struggle and failure, doubt and pain, shame and envy, longing and desire can all be held within the loving gaze of a tender and compassionate God.

Practical implications

What are the implications of all this for the work of missional communities and their leaders? I hope that much of it might be simply to inspire and embolden those communities to find ways of expressing the sacrament of confession in the fullest way possible and to see it as a vitally important dimension of mission and ministry. Related to this, they might discern and support those leaders who are gifted in listening and put them forward for further training. Although there are many ways leaders might use the insight expressed here by enhancing their listening and deepening their conviction about the meaning and place of confession, it is important that the specific expertise and role of spiritual direction be understood and valued and used.

With regard being used, it would seem to me imperative that leaders of missional communities should find for themselves a spiritual director with understanding in the gifts and challenges of pioneer ministry. But also, they would do well to find one or two spiritual directors who might form, very loosely speaking, part of their team; spiritual directors with interest and skill in working with people outside of the Church or with Christians struggling to move forward.

As an example, I was called upon by Ian Mobsby, the founder and former Priest Missioner of the Moot Community in London. He invited me to support a number of those in the leadership team over the years but also to find other spiritual directors to support members of the community. Ian was clear and, I think, exceptional in his commitment to this sort of support for both his leaders but also for the young, unchurched or de-churched in his community. I believe that it made a great difference to the growing maturity of that community.

Postscript

In conclusion, it must be said that while confession is traditionally understood to be about 'struggles and sin', it might also be about the closely held secrets of potential, aspiration and vision which are also buried for fear of failure or rejection. To invite others to come out of hiding means allowing the guilt and shame to be dispelled but also the God-given desires and creativity to flourish. We must remember that to be fully human even in our beauty takes a lot of courage; even this makes us vulnerable. We'd often rather 'play small' than step into the open and risk the full experience of being who we are in a world of jealousy and judgement, competition and superficial standards.

To absolve means to set free. True confession will always be to this end, whether confession of hurts or wrongs, shame or guilt, vision or beauty. Confession, mission and spiritual direction all share this ministry; to bring the good news of God's love and to set people free to be all they were created to be in Christ. In so doing, we offer our small but potent part in pursuing peace and reconciliation in a conflicted and divided world.

> Swallowing his pride, the aristocrat approached the elder with an open heart, sharing the struggles, failures and sins he

had never allowed anyone else to know. At once, he received the words he had been seeking.

Notes

1 Adapted from Mark Barrett, *Crossing: Reclaiming the Landscape of our Lives*, Morehouse Publishing, New York, 2008, p. 59.

2 James Keegan SJ, quoted at www.sdiworld.org/find-a-spiritual-director/what-is-spiritual-direction.

16

Picking up the Pieces: Reconciliation and Community in a Fragmented World

SIMON SUTCLIFFE

As I write this chapter, I suspect a divine sense of humour at work. A Methodist writing about the sacrament of reconciliation? But we are sacramental. Most local churches celebrate the Eucharist (usually called The Lord's Supper or Holy Communion) on a Sunday once a month (there also might be a midweek regular Communion service). This is more to do with historical accident and church polity than a suspicion of sacraments in themselves. That said, Methodists generally only recognize two sacraments – baptism and Eucharist. So writing about the sacrament of reconciliation in a Methodist missional community is truly pushing the boundaries of our understanding of church.

The truth is, however, reconciliation is happening: we are Methodist and there is a sacramental quality to what is happening to us as a community.

The *truth* about what happened

Truth is a complicated thing. It begins at a single point: a moment, an utterance, an event; but any articulation of that truth will soon be bound up in interpretation clouded by context. Even if we could identify The Truth – any telling of it – any truth claim will always be constructed. What lies behind this chapter is a Truth, but it must remain veiled to the reader because any expression of it will only ever be *my truth*, my construction of what happened. So all the reader needs to know about this *true story* is this:

Once upon a time there was a church plant . . .
after a number of years there wasn't . . .
people fell out . . .
and that left people hurting . . .
and then, through the oddest of circumstances . . .
my path crossed theirs . . .

The pixilated characters that play out this drama in the background of this text are real, their stories are true, but they are not mine to tell. What I can offer is a theological reflection on how this disparate, once-community, reformed and became the bedrock of relationships that sustains my faith – my closest friends.

Picking up the pieces . . . the story of immerse

I've already noted my inability to share the pains and hurts of those saints who God placed in my way, but I can share how we began to put it right. In the end it turns out not to be overly complicated, it just takes time, persistence and is often accompanied by tears!

When immerse (the missional community I am a part of) first started to gather, we tried to do what we thought we knew worked. Some of us had experienced, and those who hadn't had heard, that large churches had lively music and a big attractional worship event. We were fortunate that we had some truly accomplished musicians and access to technology that meant we could be live and loud!

But it never quite felt right, and on reflection, why would it? Why would ten people in a room, struggling both emotionally and mentally, be able to worship in that style?

We carried on, struggling with what we knew.

After about a year of this, we decided that for Lent we would do something different. Each week we read one of the Gospel accounts of Jesus' temptation in the wilderness. We read it slowly and deliberately and tried to emulate something of the discipline of *Lectio Divina* (a traditional 'spiritual exercise' that enables a person or group to meditate on a biblical text). After this, we went into the kitchen and ate soup together.

Throughout the centuries of the Church, Lent has been a time of reflection and discernment. We discovered something that particular Lent, something that was hiding in plain sight, something we all know because in almost any other context we instinctively practise it.

Community happens around the table, over a cup of coffee, a glass of wine or a meal; and, more importantly, the kitchen is often the arena for significant conversations to be had, and decisions to be made.

So after Easter, we carried on.

We met weekly to eat and monthly to worship.

When we had to move venue, we carried on.

Sometimes there might only be three of us, other times 20. The kids on the estate came to know that we ate together on a Sunday afternoon and they would all turn up for pizza and hot chocolate. Then weeks would go by without us seeing them until they reappeared.

The number of people who came was not as important as the space that was created. If we knew people were unable to make it we would work hard to ensure someone, even if they were on their own, came to eat.

This is how reconciliation happened: this was our sacrament and the kitchen became our confessional.

Reconciliation: a Methodist understanding

In order to see how this became for us a sacrament of reconciliation, it is necessary to say something about how the nature and status of the sacrament of reconciliation is understood in the Church. This is not the chapter for a detailed historical and technical examination of the sacrament. Those interested could have a cursory read of Joseph Martos' *Doors to the Sacred*[1] or the small but wonderfully lucid work of Monika K. Hellwig, *Sign of Reconciliation and Conversion*.[2]

What can be said about the sacrament of reconciliation is that it has had a complex and often difficult airing in the Church. As you read through journal articles and textbooks about the sacrament you soon discover that most Roman Catholic scholars see the sacrament in crisis. The sacrament seems to have found itself caught between two tensions that either elevate it to the position of *mystery*, utterly unfathomable by human minds, or reduce it to an anachronistic gesture that has been outmoded by the *well-being* genre of a postmodern world. To that extent the sacrament and theme of reconciliation has been lost to an overly personalized sense of self: either God is the only forgiver and, therefore, any sense of sin and forgiveness only needs to happen between me and the divine; or I am the true victim of my own brokenness and, therefore, my ability to reconcile myself with myself is the primary benefit of reconciliation.

So where might we begin to recover a role for the sacrament of reconciliation in the Church? The obvious place to begin is with the Church!

The Church – the community of the baptized – is the place where salvation and conversion are eternal realities. By that I mean that I was not once 'saved' and will, therefore, be saved for evermore; rather my baptism marks the moment of salvation and conversion that I cannot avoid if I choose to remain in the Body of Christ. I am continually called by God to reframe and reshape my life, or to put it another way, I continually participate in my own salvation. It is true that it is only God who redeems, but the believer is continually being asked 'Are you redeemable?' and the answer to that question lies not in my actions and misdemeanours but in my capacity to show myself willing to be redeemed, changed, transformed. Nothing I do is beyond the bounds of God to be made right, but I must be willing to subject myself to such renewal. The Church, therefore, is a community where *character* and *formation* take centre ground. Who I am, and what I become as a follower of Jesus in a fractured world becomes a primary concern of the whole Church. In the Methodist tradition, we have often associated *character* and *formation* with the concept of holiness.

In the early days of the Methodist movement, John Wesley (the founder of the Methodist Church) organized new converts into 'class meetings'. These weekly meetings had 10–12 people who gathered in people's homes (usually the leaders') to be accountable to one another about their daily Christian life. Andrew Goodhead's excellent work, *A Crown and a Cross: The Rise, Development, and Decline of the Methodist Class Meeting in Eighteenth-Century England*,[3] argues that the class meeting had four overlapping functions. First, it was a place of fellowship: members accompanied one another on a common journey. Second, it was a place of conversion and discipleship. It was expected that members demonstrated, in their living, that a new life had begun. Third, the class meeting was a place of financial accountability. The class meetings were originally founded as a way of paying off building debts, but Wesley, who had a keen organizational eye, soon recognized the wider benefits of bringing people together. That said, monies were still required from members and a certain level of accountability as to how they spent the rest of their money was not uncommon. Finally, Goodhead suggests, the class meetings were a place of discipline. That included both an account of a member's own actions and the possibility of being reproved by others in the meeting.

From the earliest days of the Methodist movement, it can be seen how corporate responsibility for one another and a public account of a Christian life were essential elements of discipleship. The purpose of such an accountability was to 'build one another up in love' and to practise and develop a holiness befitting a follower of Jesus. The class meetings, as they were once practised, fell out of fashion in Methodism shortly after the death of Wesley, but their essence has remained. To be a disciplined, corporate, accountable group of believers, continually seeking to be renewed and reshaped, sits deep within Methodist DNA – and this trait emerged in a Methodist fresh expression when we least expected it.

What we discovered in immerse was that the rhythm of life we had created, of preparing food and eating together, offered us the opportunity to talk; to share concerns, to imagine possibilities and to reacquaint ourselves with the business of loving one another.

In essence, we created a class meeting: a place where we learnt to be honest with one another, where we held one another in love and to account. A place where wounds were sometimes openly visible and pain was not hidden. Phrases such as 'We don't have to be perfect to be a Christian' and 'We don't need to have it all figured out to be together' became popular. We began to find others were drawn to us because they too felt broken in some way, out of place, disjointed. It seemed our honesty about our fragility paved the way for others to be honest about theirs – a shared vulnerability where forgiveness and reconciliation become possible.

To see this process as a sacrament of reconciliation we need to return to its crisis. Part of the problem of an overly personalized sense of self is that either I don't require to confess or be offered forgiveness through a priest (after all, this is between me and God), or all I need is the forgiveness of the priest without any sense of being reconciled to anything (after all, this is about my need to be forgiven). But if we take as our starting point the Church as a place where salvation and transformation is continually being sought and received then both of these responses fall short. It is true that re-centring of self is vital to a life of Christian integrity. It is also true that God forgives those who seek it and can do so without any human agency, but I also need to be reconciled to the Church, to other human beings, and that is – without doubt – an external, human thing to do.

The word 'church' (Ekklesia) is rarely used in the Gospels but it does occur in Matthew:

> 'And I tell you, you are Peter, and on this rock I will build my church, and the gates of Hades will not prevail against it. I will give you the keys of the kingdom of heaven, and whatever you bind on earth will be bound in heaven, and

> whatever you loose on earth will be loosed in heaven.' (Matthew 16.18–19)

and later, Jesus is recorded as saying,

> 'If another member of the church sins against you, go and point out the fault when the two of you are alone. If the member listens to you, you have regained that one. But if you are not listened to, take one or two others along with you, so that every word may be confirmed by the evidence of two or three witnesses. If the member refuses to listen to them, tell it to the church; and if the offender refuses to listen even to the church, let such a one be to you as a Gentile and a tax collector. Truly I tell you, whatever you bind on earth will be bound in heaven, and whatever you loose on earth will be loosed in heaven. Again, truly I tell you, if two of you agree on earth about anything you ask, it will be done for you by my Father in heaven. For where two or three are gathered in my name, I am there among them.' (Matthew 18.15–20)

In the first passage Peter, who recognizes Jesus as the Messiah, the saviour, is given the Keys of the Kingdom, and with that comes the authority to *loose* and *bind*. Later, in chapter 18 that same language of *loosing* and *binding* is used of the whole Church. Peter clearly has a unique and precious place in the forming, keeping and growth of the Church, but that authority to loose and bind belongs to the Church entire. Not only that, but the authority bestowed on the Church is ratified in heaven. This is crucial, because it means that reconciliation happens on a number of different levels. As I have already mentioned, the reconciliation within myself (personal) and with God (divine) is essential, but neither of those things shortcut or bypass the reconciliation that needs to occur within the church (communal). This makes absolute sense if we see the Church as the place of salvation and transformation. If the fracture – the sin – places me in such a position that I am no longer open to that saving and transforming work of God, then I set myself outside of the

Church. It is only as I am reconciled to the humanly-heavenly company of the Church that I find myself back in the flow of God's saving work.

This is what was happening in those early class meetings. Members were asked 'Do you fear the wrath to come?' (Are you open to the saving and transforming power of God?) and held to account, one to another, for their daily living, watching over one another in love and *reproving* one another where necessary. What is more, they did this weekly, they committed themselves to this kind of community and what was *loosed* or *bound* in the class meeting had the authority of heaven.

Picking up the pieces . . . in a fragmented world

We never intended to form a class meeting when immerse came together. I suspect it was so deep in our Christian experience and DNA that what emerged had traits of our inheritance. As people, who had been hurt by others, began to come together regularly to share, talk and cry we recovered our place in the community of the baptized. We found out for ourselves that forgiveness and reconciliation come personally, corporately and divinely. We discovered that being held in community with honesty and integrity is life-giving.

This might raise questions from those who come at the sacraments from a different place. What was the role of the priest? Where was the ritual act? I want to suggest that I, as an ordained Methodist presbyter, had a very simple and particular focus. My job was simply to ensure that we kept meeting. My role was to hold open the space long enough for others to begin the arduous task of relationships. To be present in the moment, to cook, to chat, to listen, and to witness. The ritual, the ongoing moment of reconciliation was in every meeting. Surely, it was just a group of friends meeting in a community centre?

Possibly?

Is it just bread, wine and water?

These things become for us more than bread, wine and water; and this gathering became for us more than eating together.

That leads us towards Eucharist (or what we would call in the Methodist tradition, The Lord's Supper). This shouldn't surprise us. In Bonhoeffer's little book *Life Together*[4] he insists that confession, one to the other, is necessary before the community can celebrate in Holy Communion. This has tended to be the experience of immerse also. Our worship has shifted over the four years of us being together towards a simple, informal, Eucharist celebrated in a small room in the community centre we call home. This is where our journey of reconciliation has taken us, and just as we are promised in the Eucharist, there is more to come.

One of the consequences of a community journeying from a place of pain is that we have to continually reassess who we believe we are called to be, as a community. This has been a complex task for us; we often share in passages of Scripture wondering how they help us deepen our identity. As relationships are recovered, reshaped and transformed, it becomes necessary to ask ourselves 'Who are we now?' On one such occasion we read the passage of Jesus feeding the 5,000. We wondered why he did it, when, as the Gospels record, he was tempted in the desert to turn the stones into bread and he refused. Our attention was drawn, though, to another part of the story. At the end, when all had been fed (and were full), the fragments were collected in 12 baskets. We knew this was significant and wondered . . .

What if God calls immerse to be in the spaces of the fragments? What if everything we have gone through together means that we rejoice in the bounteous, generous giving of Jesus but we locate ourselves with the ones 'left over' – the ones who don't quite fit, those who are discarded when the world is 'full'? We are still working out what this means, as we are only four years old, but we know it means something. We recognize that a community that owns its vulnerability offers opportunities to those who are fragile. We are just beginning to realize, although we have never spoken of it in these terms before, that reconciliation does not end with us, it begins there. Just as all sacraments transcend any particular time or place, so the work God has begun in us here is for the benefit of the whole created order. Our task is to continue to be a reconciling community that draws others into God's reconciling way. This is what Methodists understand as holiness, to practise a way of living that is shaped by the life, death and resurrection of Jesus in order to bring about transformation in a fragmented world.

This is the story of immerse . . . so far.

Notes

1 Joseph Martos, *Doors to the Sacred: A Historical Introduction to Sacraments in the Christian Church*, SCM Press, London, 1981.

2 Monika K. Hellwig, *Sign of Reconciliation and Conversion: The Sacrament of Penance for Our Times*, Michael Glazier, Wilmington, 1982.

3 Andrew Goodhead, *A Crown and a Cross: The Rise, Development, and Decline of the Methodist Class Meeting in Eighteenth-Century England*, Wipf & Stock Publishers, Oregon, 2010.

4 Dietrich Bonhoeffer, *Life Together*, SCM Press, Norwich, 2015.

Afterword

MICHAEL MOYNAGH

In this concluding chapter, I want to suggest that the Church is relational by nature, and that the sacraments arise out of these relationships and make them possible. If this is the case, then fresh expressions of church are called to keep asking, 'How are the sacraments feeding our relationships? Are we being summoned to celebrate them in new ways that would enhance the fruitfulness of these relationships? Might a sacrament that is not yet part of our life nourish and strengthen the relationships that make us an expression of the church?'

Some origins

Sacraments have emerged from the life of the Church. In the case of baptism and Holy Communion, how this happened is not always clear.[1] Yet we know enough to understand the Last Supper narratives 'not as a curious quirk of ritual practice instituted by Jesus in isolation but as an original expression and interpretation of familiar and widespread meal customs.'[2] Communal meals were the original setting for the breaking of bread (Acts 2.46), which evolved into Holy Communion.

Breaking the bread became an opportunity to remember and encounter Jesus. It happened within individual gatherings. Yet because it was practised, it seems, by all these Christian communities, it became a source of identity for the Church as a whole. It also had a missional dimension. New Testament scholar Rita Finger reminds us how city dwellings in the ancient world were packed together, with no glass windows to shut out the noise. Neighbours could hear what was going on.[3] This was literally *public* worship. Thus Communion arose from believers' relationships with God directly, with one another in their immediate Christian community, with the wider church – 'this is what other communities are doing and so we must do the same' (cf. 1 Corinthians 11.23ff.), and with the world.

Baptism may have emerged from ritual washing in everyday settings, such as before meals. By the time of Jesus, these everyday washings were becoming opportunities to extend the holiness associated with the temple into daily life.[4] However, John's baptism of repentance went beyond this and 'was undoubtedly perceived as doing something unique'.[5] It was a reorientation towards God within Judaism. Likewise, the baptism practised by Jesus's disciples, while adding belief in Jesus and participation in the life of the Spirit, was initially a ritual of renewal within Judaism. Only as Gentiles increasingly became followers of Jesus did baptism become the means of entry into a movement that was beginning to transcend Judaism.

As with the Lord's Supper, this early development of baptism had strongly relational origins. It arose from believers' relationships with God directly (people were baptized in the name of the Father, Son and Holy Spirit – Matthew 28.19), with the whole Church (it quickly became a rite of entry into the entire community of Christ's followers), with one another in the immediate Christian fellowship (it normally occurred, as far as we can tell, in the context of a gathering or, as in the case of Lydia, the nucleus of one – Acts 16.13ff.), and with the world as the Church attracted newcomers.

Thus baptism and Holy Communion, the paradigmatic sacraments if you like, were not afterthoughts added to the Church. From the very beginning, they were connected to and arose from the relationships at the heart of the Church. This matters. The sacraments are essential to the Church not as strange rituals that must be added in, but as aspects of the Church's life that belong to the very nature, the relational nature, of the Church.

The relational essence of the Church

However, the Church's fundamental nature has not always been understood in relational terms. For centuries it has been largely conceived in terms of certain practices. When practices like the word, sacraments and ministry were present, 'a church' was said to exist. Over the past half century, this emphasis on practices has been supplemented by the idea of the Church as a pilgrim people. The ecumenical consensus now holds that the essence of the Church is a fellowship (or community) of people who adopt certain practices.[6]

This consensus is not without problems. In particular, the relationship between the fellowship of people and these practices is left undefined. For example, do practices like Holy Communion and baptism serve the people in ways that allow these practices to be substantially modified? Or are the practices relatively fixed, so that the people have to learn, as it were, how to fit into them? Or is it a bit of both? In which case, where does the balance lie?

I would like to suggest that we understand the essence of the Church in a slightly different way. Fundamentally, the Church comprises four sets of interlocking relationships focused on Jesus – with God directly in prayer, study and worship, with the world, with the wider Church and within the fellowship. In real life, these relationships flow in and out of each other and are bound intimately together. They are separated here for descriptive purposes. All the sets of relationships should be given equal weight, not least because God is present in each of them.[7]

This relational heart of the Church echoes the Trinity. The Father's giving to the Son (Matthew 28.18) and the Son's obedience to the Father (John 8.28–9) find their counterpart in the Church's relationship with God. The Church's relationship with the world is a participation in God's mission through the Spirit. The loving interactions of the divine persons correspond to relationships within the fellowship. Relations with the whole body, which enable each gathering to influence the wider Church and be influenced by it, are the ecclesial counterpart to the – in technical language – *perichoretic* relationships within the Trinity. This includes the idea that the three divine persons are so bound up with each other, without ceasing to be distinct persons, that each person profoundly impacts the others – one affects all.[8]

These four overlapping sets of relationships also characterize the kingdom. In Revelation 21's picture of the kingdom, for example, God dwells among his peoples, which is the Godward relationship (21.3). The city consists of 'peoples' – a variety of people groups; relations within each group have their counterpart in the relations within the fellowship (each unit of the Church). Each group is part of the whole city, just as each fellowship is part of the whole Church. The city's openness to the kings and the nations outside (21.24, 26) is reflected in the Church's mission to people who are not yet within the Christian family.

This relational description of the Church accords with everyday observation. A congregation has relationships with the wider Church, with God directly in worship, study and prayer, with the world, and within the fellowship as members relate to one another. In British evangelical circles, the Church has sometimes been described as UP (relations with God), IN (relations within the church) and OUT (relations with the world). The trouble is that IN conflates two sets of relationships – between the fellowship and the wider Church, and within the fellowship. Because the latter is more immediate to church members, it is easy for the 'wider church' relationships to be pushed to the background. Seeing the Church as fundamentally four sets of relationships, all of equal importance, helps to avoid this.

Essential practices

Alongside the relational essence of the Church, it might be helpful to describe certain practices as being essential to the Church. What is the essence of something and what is essential to it need not be the same. A referee is essential for a soccer match, but is not the essence of the game. A charity is required to have an annual general meeting, but this is not the heart of its charitable activities. In the 'West', a knife and fork are essential for eating, but are not the essence of the meal.

Likewise in the Church, certain practices are essential for the four interlocking sets of relationships to exist and flourish, but they are not the relational essence of the Church. These practices make it possible for the ecclesial match to be played, if you like, but they are not the essence of the game. What these practices are and how they should be expressed continues to be much debated. In the reformed tradition, essential practices would include the word, ministry and sacraments, though which sacraments (in addition to baptism and Holy Communion) would again be a matter of debate.

The idea of essentials adds an important nuance to the distinction traditionally made between practices that are the 'esse' – the essence – of the Church, and those that are for the 'bene esse' – the well-being – of the Church. The notion of essentials splits the Church's 'esse' into two components – the Church's relational essence and practices that are essential for this relational essence to exist and thrive. Thus we can speak of the Church's esse (its relational essence), the Church's essentials (which make the relational essence possible), and the Church's bene esse (the well-being of the church).

This distinction between essence and essentials is not explicit in the tradition, but it can be said to be implicit – in tune with the tradition's best instincts. First, by accenting the Church's relationships, the distinction is true to the relational picture of the Church in the New Testament. New Testament imagery of the Church, for example, is strongly relational – the household of God, the vine and the branches, and many more. In his classic *Images of Church in the New Testament*, Paul Minear[9] described four controlling images – the people of God, the new creation (which includes the restoration of fractured relationships), the fellowship of faith and the body of Christ. All are relational pictures.

Second, the distinction works with the ecumenical consensus that the Church is a pilgrim people. If persons exist in and through their relationships – a truism for theologians and social scientists – 'people' must include the relationships that make them a people. To speak of the Church as a people is to acknowledge that relationships are central to the Church. Distinguishing between the essence and the essentials of the Church allows this recognition to be stated unambiguously. It takes the recent shift in understanding the Church from institution to koinonia (community) to its logical conclusion.

Third, the distinction between essence and essentials takes intensely seriously the tradition's emphasis on certain practices being crucial to the Church's life. The distinction does not foreclose the debate on what these practices are and the form they should take, but it does recognize that the Church could not exist without these practices. If there were no word, no leadership and no sacraments, for example, the four sets of relationships that constitute the Church could not flourish. Essential practices are the Spirit's means for establishing and growing these relationships.

In particular, the view here has an explicit place for those who believe that baptism and Holy Communion bring the Church into existence. Not everyone holds that view, but those who do could argue that being essential for (but not the essence of) something is consistent with it. A feature of many 'essentials' is that they precede 'essences'. A knife and fork are on the table before the meal is served. The match does not begin till the referee blows the whistle. Because they are essentials, they are *pre*requisites. Just as the referee brings the match into being, those of a more Catholic persuasion can argue that baptism and Holy Communion bring the Church into existence.

Sacraments as servants

Fourthly, and especially important, the distinction between essence and essentials allows us to start describing the connection between the two. The essentials are not ends in themselves. As John Drane notes in his chapter, there is an extensive literature about sacraments, 'much of it relating to issues that have more to do with power politics than with theology'. A relational perspective puts some checks and balances around the politics. It encourages practices to be tested against the bar of relationships – by asking for example, 'How far does the way we usually celebrate Holy Communion help this group of people to grow in their relationship with God, with each other, with the world and with the wider body?' When practices are in dispute, relationships provide a touchstone for what is ultimately important in the body. Disagreements will be framed by the need to maintain health in all four sets of ecclesial relations.

Earlier chapters in the book illustrate something of how the Spirit works through the sacraments to build up the Church's four sets of relationships. Susan Blagden and Philip Roderick, for instance, describe how the Contemplative Fire community re-imagined 'a fresh expression of baptism'. Community members' relationships with each other were deepened, it seems, as they did theology together. So too their direct relationships with God as they examined Scripture. Their relations with the wider Church were strengthened by taking advice from the bishop, who was a source of wisdom. The 18-month preparation period can be seen as a missional activity, drawing the three baptismal candidates deeper into the kingdom, which was part of the community's relationships with the world.

Using baptism as an example, Bishop Jonathan Clark argues that people need not wait till after they have come to faith to experience the sacraments: the sacraments can appropriately be part of their journeys to faith. He calls for an 'open font', a re-coupling of baptism with preaching the gospel, so that – following the example in Acts 2.41 – as people are convicted by the word they can respond by being baptized there and then.

He notes that Peter's response to the crowd's question at Pentecost, 'What shall we do?' was to urge them to 'Repent and be baptized.' Baptism is an act of turning to God. At the same time, it is entry into the whole body of Christ. 'It is the sacrament of belonging at least as much as it is the sacrament of believing.' This entry cannot be theoretical. It must be embodied in a specific community of disciples. Baptism thus involves and strengthens the four ecclesial relationships.

The same is true of Holy Communion. In Lucy Moore's account of Communion within Messy Church, she quotes her colleague, Martyn Payne, saying that the mission element might lie in helping not-yet believers in the community to take a step towards Jesus. Communion gives the Church's relationships with the world, through Messy Church, an evangelistic edge. In Bishop Graham Cray's phrase, it is 'a public invitation to dine'.

Karen Ward describes how in her small community in Seattle, this public invitation became a weekly event in response to spiritual seekers' desire for an experience of spirituality as part of their journeys. She notes how encountering the Holy Spirit unsettles people, which encourages them to explore more. 'This unsettling activity of the Holy Spirit is again beyond words, and is the beginning of a yearning for the sacred as the beginning of sacramentality.' She has a number of friends who came to faith through experiencing Holy Communion and were subsequently ordained.

Lucy draws attention to how Communion in the context of a meal is a 'means to encounter the love of God and for God to act in ways beyond our control'. As well as strengthening this direct relationship with God, Communion 'can be a time of looking outwards to feel a connection with other churches'. As Bishop Graham reminds us, for the believers involved, Holy Communion renews their Christian identities.

Lucy graphically describes how Communion can also strengthen relationships within the fellowship. A well-filled table 'creates community, it fosters belonging, it shouts out silently, "You matter! You are worth it! You are one of us! We are together!"' This is echoed by Kim Hartshorne, who recounts one young man in her Upper Room Community describing what Holy Communion meant to him: 'We get to join in and be part of the team. We are together, we do this together'.

The sacrament of confession likewise reinforces the Church's four interlocking sets of relationships. Penitents are drawn closer to God through prayerful repentance and the assurance of forgiveness. Adrian Chatfield describes his sense of an action completed by God. Relations within the fellowship are deepened since confession arises from 'a community of grace which does not hold us hostage to our past'. Confession and absolution intensify penitents' belonging to a particular type of community, one defined by grace.

Confession also strengthens relations with the Church at large, which has authorized the person to hear confession and, if some form of liturgy is used, has given that liturgy to the gathering. The absolution carries the authority of God as mediated by the wider Church. Finally, when sins have occurred in the world this relationship is restored. To help penitents follow Jesus in the world, the sacrament may include 'an appropriate repayment, a rebuilding of a kingdom damaged by what we have done'.

As Julie Dunstan points out, spiritual direction can open up the sacrament of confession. Spiritual direction enriches the Church's relations with the world when it is a ministry to people on the edge of the Church. They can be enabled to (re)connect with God and receive his forgiveness. The authority of the whole Church can play an important part in this deepening of their relationship with God. 'absolution delivered, if you will, from a visible representative of the Church can speak powerfully against the condemning authority figures from the past, residing inside the despair of so many.'

Julie has provided spiritual direction to some of the leaders and members of Moot community in London, and sensed 'that it made a great difference to the growing maturity of that community'. When it is widely welcomed by members of a gathering, spiritual direction can be the Spirit's vehicle to give relationships between them a Jesus shape.

Simon's Sutcliffe's account of what his Methodist community, immerse, learnt about the sacrament of reconciliation offers another example of how the Spirit can inhabit the sacraments to build up the four sets of ecclesial relationships. He notes that the sacrament involves reconciliation with God. It occurs within the immediate Christian community, which is strengthened when members help each other to be reconciled. As members are reconciled, the community becomes a means of reconciliation for others and has a responsibility to take this reconciliation into the world. In immerse, the wider Church played a significant role. Members learned from the precedent set by the eighteenth-century Methodist classes, in which participants confessed their sins and were assured of God's forgiveness.

Relational discernment

If the sacraments are avenues for the Spirit to nourish and transform the relationships of the Church, a priority for fresh expressions should be to prayerfully discern the form these sacraments should take so that they can be suitable pathways for the Spirit. This raises all sorts of questions! The one I would like to highlight is the importance of a relational approach to discernment. In God's grace, discernment will involve the Church's four overlapping sets of relationships. This is because deciding how the sacraments can best serve the essence of the Church is a task best undertaken by the essence of the Church.

Ideally, each set of relationships should be given equal weight, though in practice the traditions of denominations, networks and individual congregations will qualify this and flesh out how it works. Balance is important because if discernment is left mainly to the church hierarchy, representing the Church at large, the inclination will be to define valid worship in terms of what already exists. Hierarchies tend to have a vested interest in the status quo. Equally, if discernment is left primarily to each gathering, insufficient attention may be paid to the wider Church. Worship may be impoverished by being too local in its imagination. Further, if discernment is left mainly to people who are new to the Church, they may lack the wisdom and the breadth of vision that Christian experience makes possible. Finally, if discernment is left principally to direct encounters with God such as prophetic words, untested subjective opinion may creep in.

Balanced discernment allows the Spirit to use each set of ecclesial relations to challenge the others. It involves mutual accountability. It should be undertaken, therefore, prayerfully in the light of Scripture, having a view to the missional context, shared within the gathering, and involving dialogue with the wider body. This is not a simple device for discovering God's will. It will often be messy precisely because it is faithful to the Church's relational nature. Relationships *are* messy!

The goal of balanced discernment offers a counterweight to the traditions of denominations, networks and local churches. These traditions gravitate in different directions, reflecting which set of ecclesial relationships are given priority. More catholic traditions, for example, tend to pull discernment towards the ecclesial hierarchy, representing the wider Church. In contrast are traditions that locate discernment in the congregation. Liberationist traditions emphasize shared discernment with marginalized groups. Pentecostals stress the role of direct words from God. In practice, traditions seek some sort of compromise between these emphases, but with a bias towards one (or two). The goal of balanced discernment challenges the innate bias of each tradition.

For example, in the Church of England, authority in matters of worship lies with the bishop, whose authority is shared with the minister of the local church, whose authority in turn is shared with the laity. Traditionally, local discretion was highly constrained by liturgies authorized nationally, which reinforced the hierarchical nature of discernment. Recently, however, greater discretion and creativity at a local level have been encouraged.[10] The ideal of balanced discernment would nudge this further by an additional loosening of central control.

In such an event, diocesan liturgical groups could help to prevent the pendulum swinging too far towards congregationalism. The national Liturgical Commission has encouraged these groups to seek out and promote good practice. It suggests that congregations invite a skilled individual or small group to observe their worship and make suggestions.[11] Under the authority of the bishop and drawing on central guidance, such groups could foster local innovation, facilitate the cross-fertilization of good practice between congregations (including new ones), encourage them to visit and learn from each other, make available to them liturgical expertise and resources from the Anglican tradition, and promote the ideal of balanced discernment.

As a growing number of new ecclesial communities in particular push the boundaries of accepted practice, experimentation can be helpfully framed by a policy of generous exceptions.[12] This should not be a means to keep new communities at arms-length from the mainstream – 'We'll generously permit them to be exceptions so that we don't have to change.' Rather, generous exceptions can be Spirit-given opportunities to test and learn from innovations. Exceptions enable the Church to ask, 'Lord, is this the direction in which you are now leading us?' They are rooted in caution about an over-realized eschatology: the Church's current practices are not to be identified too closely with the kingdom. God's reign is *coming* – it has not completely arrived – and so today's practices cannot fully reflect the kingdom. Through generous exceptions, the Spirit can continually reform the Church and keep it moving towards its ultimate destination.

Conclusion

The sacraments are gifts from God to draw us closer to him in worship, study and prayer, to each other, to the world and to the wider Communion of saints. They are vehicles through which the Spirit builds up these four sets of relationships – relationships that lie at the heart of the Church. In other words, the sacraments are servants of these relationships. This means that those in authority must be careful not to insist on their definitions of good practice in relation to the sacraments in ways that leave other people disempowered. The attempt to impose uniformity risks becoming 'a temptation to pride, which makes a group in power pretend to possess God fully and impose limits on how God is revealed in "other" cultures'.[13] If the sacraments are to serve all the ecclesial relationships, all these relationships must be prayerfully involved in discerning the form the sacraments should take.

Notes

1 Paul F. Bradshaw, *The Search for the Origins of Christian Worship*, SPCK, London, 2002.

2 Andrew B. McGowan, *Ancient Christian Worship*, Baker Academic, 2014, Grand Rapids, p. 27

3 Rita Finger, 2007, *Of Widows and Meals: Communal Meals in the Book of Acts*, Eerdmans, Grand Rapids, 2007, p. 242.

4 McGowan, *Ancient Christian Worship*, p. 136.

5 McGowan, *Ancient Christian Worship*, p. 138

6 *The Church: Towards a Common Vision*, World Council of Churches, Geneva, 2013.

7 The argument is developed more fully in my *Church in Life*, SCM Press, London, forthcoming 2017, chapter 12.

8 Miroslav Volf, *After Our Likeness: The Church as the Image of the Trinity*, Eerdmans, Grand Rapids, 1998, p. 209.

9 Paul Minear, *Images of Church in the New Testament*, Westminster John Knox Press, Louisville, 1970.

10 Church of England Liturgical Commission, *Transforming Worship: Living the New Creation*, General Synod, 2007.

11 Church of England Liturgical Commission, *Transforming Worship*, pp. 23–4, 26.

12 Lindsay Urwin, 'What is the Role of Sacramental Ministry in Fresh Expressions of Church?', in Steve Croft (ed.), *Mission-shaped Questions*, Church House Publishing, London, 2008, p. 35.

13 François K. Lumbala, *Celebrating Christ in Africa: Liturgy and Inculturation*, Orbis, Maryknoll, 1998, p. 6.